# Key Words in Islam

# Key Words in Islam

Ron Geaves

Georgetown University Press / Washington, D.C.

As of January 1, 2007, 13-digit ISBN numbers will replace the current 10-digit system.
Paperback: 978-1-58901-124-3

Georgetown University Press, Washington, D.C.

**Library of Congress Cataloging-in-Publication Data**

Geaves, Ron.
  Key words in Islam / Ron Geaves.
     p. cm.
  ISBN 1-58901-124-4 (alk. paper)
  1. Islam—Encyclopedias. 2. Islam—Dictionaries. 3. Islam—Terminology.
I. Title.
  BP40.G396 2006
  297.03—dc22
                                    2006006888

This book is printed on acid-free paper meeting the requirements of the American National Standard for Permanence in Paper for Printed Library Materials.

13 12 11 10 09 08 07 06    9 8 7 6 5 4 3 2
First printing

Printed in Great Britain

# Contents

# PREFACE

During the course of teaching a number of religions in four higher education institutions, one common feature has been the number of students who have told me that they found the mastering of religious terminology in so many unknown languages and involving unfamiliar concepts to be the most daunting part of the module. In view of this, the *Key Words* series was created to provide a glossary of terms for five religions.

The religions have been chosen to reflect the main traditions that are studied both in school and at university in the English-speaking world. One glossary also contains the key specialist terminology used in the academic study of religion. It is hoped that the glossaries will prove to be useful and informative resources for anyone studying religion up to undergraduate level, but that they will also provide a fascinating pool of information for anyone interested in religious practice or belief, whether for the purpose of gaining qualifications or simply in the personal pursuit of knowledge. Each glossary therefore provides an exhaustive exploration of religious terminology in a way that is accessible but also provides an overall in-depth understanding of the religious tradition.

Although Islam is now provided with its own separate book, even so the glossary's completion is arbitrary as each religion covered by the *Key Words* series is a conceptual framework for viewing the world that commands a vast vocabulary. This is true of Islam, which is a fully developed religious tradition over 1400 years old and represents considerable religious diversity and a global reach from China to Europe, with minority communities in North and South America and Australasia. The primary religious language of Islam is Arabic, the language of the *Qur'an*, but other languages, such as Persian, Urdu, and Turkish, provide comprehensive terminologies of their own. I have restricted the glossary to Arabic terms, although occasionally I have provided Urdu words where I felt that they offered something unique. These reflect both my own scholarly interests and the numerical dominance of South-Asian Muslims in the British Muslim community. My choice of terms has been determined by school and undergraduate curricula, and the length of each definition has been dictated by the fact that this is a glossary and not a specialist religious dictionary. Inevitably, however, some concepts and persons involved more than a short passage in order to clarify their significance and highlight their importance within the world of their respective religion. Some terms reflect my own interests as a scholar, especially those that belong largely in the world of popular religion, more familiar in village vernaculars than in various forms of orthodoxies. I have also decided to transliterate the terms into the English alphabet without diacritics. Although this may irritate the specialist scholar, especially those whose work is textual study, it remains part of the spirit of the original *Continuum Glossary of Religious Terms*, which was to provide acceptable variant spellings to non-specialists.

Finally, I would like to thank Catherine Barnes, whose patience and support has been remarkable; Janet Joyce who provided the original opportunity for this project to grow from its inception to completion; and Continuum for providing the means for the glossaries to appear in their various editions.

**Abbasid**    A dynasty of Caliphs that ruled from Baghdad and were descendents of an uncle of Muhammad, Muttalib Ibn Hashim. The Abbasids joined with the followers of ALI, the Prophet's son-in-law, to make a stronger claim to the leadership of the Muslims than the ruling UMAYYADS. Under the leadership of Abu al-Abbas, they ousted the Umayyads in 750, promising a return to religious orthodoxy combined with theocracy and drawing upon the support of non-Arab Muslims and the SHI'A. Their dynasty ruled until 1258 when they were destroyed by the Mongols. In this period there was an extraordinary flowering of Muslim culture and the development of the mystical path of the SUFIS.

**Abd**    *Lit. a slave or a servant.* It is used to denote the status of a Muslim who is obedient to the will of ALLAH by following His command-ments as laid down for all humanity in the QUR'AN. It follows on from Islam which means surrender. The highest ideal of Islam is to be the servant or slave of God, entirely submitted to His Will.

**Abduh, Muhammad**    (1845–1905) A Muslim reformer influenced by Jamal al-Din AFGHANI. Although a traditionally trained scholar of Islam, he argued that revelation and science were not incompatible with each other. He saw faith and reason as operating in independent spheres and therefore not in conflict. He enjoined Muslims to maintain their traditional faith but to develop their knowledge in other spheres of learning. He has influenced contemporary Muslims by his powerful argument that Islam was the only religion that actively calls upon

1

human beings to investigate nature and utilize reason. He argued that reason and faith had to work hand in hand with each other to benefit humankind. (*See also* SAYYID AHMAD; KHAN)

**Abu Bakr**   The first Caliph of Islam who succeeded the Prophet in the leadership of the Muslim community after his death in 632 and ruled until his own death in 634. Abu Bakr was the Prophet's father-in-law and one of the first three or four to accept the Prophet and the message of Islam. He was known for his piety and is believed to have compiled the first QUR'AN by collecting all the verses and placing them in one book. The NAQSHBANDI SUFI TARIQA regards Abu Bakr as the founder of their line of SHAIKHS. The Caliphate of Abu Bakr was riven by war between the tribes that had accepted Islam and those that had not. However, Muslim historians believe that the Riddah wars were fought against tribes that had already offered their oath of allegiance to the Prophet but later seceded and followed false prophets and gods. (*See also* AL-KHALIFA-UR-RASHIDUN)

**Abu Hanifa**   (d. 767) The founder of the HANAFI School of jurisprudence that developed in Iraq and went on to become the largest of the schools of law in the Muslim world. It was accepted as the official school of the OTTOMAN empire and still remains the dominant school in the Indian subcontinent. Abu Hanifa was a merchant by trade but became the most influential of the Muslim jurists. He taught orally, but his work was collected by one of his followers named Abu Yusef. Abu Hanifa emphasized the role of QIYAS or analogical deduction but also acknowledged the role of independent reasoning in deducing law from the Revelation. (*See also* FIQH; IJTIHAD)

**Adab**   The term refers to ideal behaviour or habit and refers to the practice of modelling an ideal Muslim life on the behaviour and habits of the Prophet. It is used by SUFIS to describe the practice of followers modelling themselves on the behaviour of their particular SHAIKH and to describe spiritual or ritual practices unique to the TARIQA. Adab may consist of wearing the same style of clothing or even carrying the same kind of stick as the Shaikh. It is hoped that by imitating the habits of the holy man, his piety and closeness to Allah will also be imbibed.

**Adam**   The father of the human race and the first prophet of Allah. Islam has no concept of original sin and the Fall as in mainstream Christianity. Although Adam and Eve make a mistake and disobey God they are both later reconciled after begging for forgiveness. The moment of reconciliation is believed to have taken place on a hill near MAKKAH and Muslims re-enact the reconciliation of Adam and Eve ritually in the annual pilgrimage to Makkah known as the HAJJ.

**Adat**   The local customs of a particular culture that has been converted to Islam. In the SHARI'A legal system, local customs are recognized as legitimate practices unless they directly contradict the precepts of Islamic law. There is a whole body of law that deals especially with local custom. (*See also* URF)

**Adha**   The need to cling to God for protection and take refuge in the shelter of His Revelation. It also carries with it the need to escape from the clutches of Satan and ensure one's safety in the afterlife. In various forms of folk religion *adha* is associated with the practice of providing TA'WIDHS or amulets for protection from disease or evil spirits.

**Adhan / Azhan (Urdu)**   The prayer-call which is recited aloud from the MOSQUE five times a day to usher Muslims to prayer. It is said to have originated in a revelation from Allah after Muhammad had deliberated on the best way to remind human beings of their obligation to God in prayer. The Christians used bells and the Jews were believed to use the ram's horn. It was decided that the human voice was the best means. The first caller of the prayer was a black companion of the Prophet named BILAL. In Britain, the prayer-call is usually made inside the mosque so as not to disturb the surrounding non-Muslim community. In translation the prayer-call is as follows: *Allah is Great (four times); I testify that there is no god but Allah (twice); I testify that Muhammad is Allah's messenger (twice); Come to prayer (twice); Come to success (twice); Prayer has begun (twice); Allah is Great (twice); There is no god but Allah (once).* (*See also* SALAT; ALLAHU AKBAR)

**Afghani, Jamal al-Din**   (1839–97) An influential nineteenth-century reformer who cautioned Muslims to unite against the dominance of

Western power and culture, he also argued that there was nothing in Islam that was opposed to the discoveries of science and technology. He urged Muslims to leave their mediaeval mindset and begin to meet the demands of modern society. (*See also* MUHAMMAD ABDUH; SAYYID AHMAD KHAN)

**Ahl al-Bait**   The household of the Prophet, especially ALI and FATIMA (the daughter of the Prophet) and his two grandsons, HUSAIN and HASAN. Although held in very high regard by all Muslims, the SHI'A hold the immediate family and their descendents in deep reverence. They believe that the bloodline of the Prophet is endowed with spiritual power that gives them some of the authority of the Prophet himself. Ali and Husain are particularly revered.

**Ahl al-Hadith**   A nineteenth-century reform movement founded by Sayyid Nazi Hussein (d. 1902), who studied with Muhammad Ishaq, the grandson of the famous Indian theologian and mystic, Shah WALIALLAH. The Ahl al-Hadith is extremely conservative and opposed to all Muslim mysticism. Most of their members are high-class and they have never become as successful as DEOBAND, the other great school founded by successors of Shah Waliallah. Birmingham is the central headquarters of the Ahl al-Hadith in Britain. In recent times they have allied themselves with the Middle-Eastern movement known as the Salafis.

**Ahl al-Kitab**   *Lit. the people of the book.* Used to refer to Jews and Christians who are also special communities that have resulted from being chosen by Allah as recipients of a prophet and a revealed scripture. There are several references in the QUR'AN to the status of Jews and Christians. For example: *Those who believe in the Qur'an, those who follow the Jewish scriptures, and the Sabians and the Christians, and who believe in Allah and the Last Day, and work righteousness, on them shall be no fear, nor shall they grieve (5:69).* In Muslim societies, the People of the Book were given privileged status and according to Muslim law (SHARI'A), marriage is permissible to a Christian or a Jew. In India, it was decided for pragmatic reasons that the early scriptures of the Hindus, such as the *Upanishads*, were monotheistic and therefore allowed for a tolerant attitude towards the Hindu majority.

**Ahl as-Sunna wa Jamaat**   The majority of traditional SUNNI Muslims as opposed to the SHI'A. However, in the contemporary Muslim world there is a fierce debate about who can be considered to be a real Sunni. The WAHABIS claim that they are the real Sunnis, but traditional Muslims who have always regarded the SUFIS with honour, and used the Prophet for his intercession believing that he has special powers to know the Unseen, are beginning to rally behind the title of Ahl as-Sunna wa-Jamaat. (*See also* ISTIGHATHA)

**Ahmadiya / Ahmadiyya**   A movement founded in the subcontinent by Mirza Ghulam Ahmad (1835–1908) whose members believed him to be the promised MAHDI. The movement divided as there were some followers who took a more eclectic line and associated their founder with Jesus and Krishna. The belief in the pre-eminence of Mirza Ghulab Ahmad has resulted in the Ahmadiya being declared non-Muslims by several states including Pakistan. With migration they have become an international movement and are known for their organizational ability.

**Ahwal**   The states of being on the path of internal purification that lead to loss of the NAFS (ego) and absorption into God (FANA) as practiced by Sufis. The states of being are contrasted to the stages through which a disciple is guided by a SHAIKH (teacher) although they are linked to them. The stages are achieved by human effort but the states of being are given by the grace of Allah. (*See also* TARIQA)

**Aisha / Aishah**   The most beloved of Muhammad's wives and the daughter of his trusted companion, ABU BAKR. She married the Prophet whilst still a young woman but when he was nearing the end of his life. After his death she became known as the 'mother of the believers' and played a prominent public role in the early years of the Muslim community and many HADITH are attributed to her. After ALI was appointed as Caliph, she led an army against him, as she did not support his claim to the Caliphate. However, she was defeated and captured. Ali treated with her with great honour but confined her to AL-MADINAH. Her dislike of Ali may have arisen from her feeling of being insulted by him when the Prophet was still alive. She had been left behind without a companion when travelling in a caravan. Ali had suggested that her virtue could no longer be trusted. (*See also* KHADIJAH)

**Ajal**   The concept that the life span of all creatures is predetermined by God. This is frequently mentioned in several passages in the QUR'AN. It is used as a warning to remind people that the time to turn towards God cannot be put off as no one knows when their allotted days will end. Pre-Islamic Arab tribes were extremely fatalistic and believed that time itself functioned in the same way to predetermine the term of life. The message of Islam replaced time with an absolute omniscient, omnipotent God. (*See also* AMR)

**Akhlaq**   *Lit. conduct, character.* It refers to a person's attitudes and ethical code. The highest exemplary behaviour is that of Muhammad. Pious Muslims try to maintain akhlaq-i Muhammadi, or the imitation of the character and ethics of the Prophet. This has been particularly marked in the SUFI tradition where the imitation of the Prophet is part of the TARIQA or spiritual discipline. (*See also* MUHAMMAD)

**al-Adawiya, Rabi'a**   (d. 801) A famous female mystic born in Basra. She was sold into slavery but released after demonstrating her piety and asceticism. She did not marry and stories abound of her one-pointed love for Allah. It is said that even in spring she did not open her shutters so that she would not be distracted from her contemplation. Rabi'a has come to epitomize loving devotion in the SUFI tradition.

**al-Adil**   *Lit. the giver of justice.* One of the descriptions of Allah that states that a central attribute of God is justice. Allah is the ultimate judge of all creation but it is also beholden on a Muslim to behave justly and dispense justice. To judge correctly is considered a religious action, but ideal Muslim governments do not exist to create laws that provide social justice, rather to maintain the laws of God already laid down in the SHARI'A. The role of Muhammad and all the prophets is to spread justice as well as to interpret the Divine Will. (*See also* QADI)

**al-Aman**     *Lit. the trustworthy.* A title that was used to describe the character of Muhammad by the people around him even before he began to receive the revelation from Allah. It is probably derived from AMIN (Amen) translated as 'so be it'. The idea being that once someone has given his or her word about something it is always fulfilled.

**al-Ashari, Abu'l Hasan**     (d. 935) The founder of the ASHARITE viewpoint that was to become victorious over other theological positions and claim the position of Muslim orthodoxy. He had originally been educated at the Mutazilite college in Basra but experienced a change of heart and adopted the anti-rationalist position of Ibn Hanbal. Al-Ashari opposed the entry of Greek thought into Islam. (*See also* HANBALI; MU'TAZILA; MURJI'ITE)

**Al-Asma al-husna**     The ninety-nine 'beautiful names of God', mentioned in the QUR'AN, which describe Allah's qualities and attributes. The ninety-nine names are used in Muslim recitation, mystical disciplines of self-purification and as words of power applied to magical or religious objects. (*See also* DHIKR; SUFI)

**Alawiya**     A generic term for two SUFI orders; the first is the Bani Alawi founded in the Hadramaut region of the Yemen. Existing as an extended family TARIQA originating in the life and teachings of Muhammad ibn Ali (1178–1255), the Bani Alawi have influenced the religious and cultural life of the Hadramaut region for generations and have spread to Indonesia, India, East Africa and Britain. The second but unconnected Sufi order consists of various movements of North Africa known as the Shadiliya Alawi. The latter were revived in the twentieth century by Shaikh Abu'l Abbas Ahmad ibn Mustafa l'Alawi (b. 1869), a prominent Algerian mystic who opened centres all over North Africa, Damascus, Aden, Palestine, Addis Adaba, Marseilles, Paris, the Hague and Britain.

**al-Azhar**   The most famous college in the Muslim world for the study of Islam. Throughout centuries many clerics have travelled to Cairo in order to study religion at the college. It is known for its conservatism and many Muslims look towards its scholars for decisions to be made on points of law. (*See also* DAR AL-ULUM; MADRASA; SHARI'A)

**al-Banna, Hasan**   (1906–49) The founder of the neo-revivalist movement, the Muslim Brotherhood in Egypt. Like Maulana MAWDUDI in Pakistan, Hasan al-Banna was committed to Islamic revolution through political and social action. He believed that he needed to create a society of like-minded, highly committed Muslims who would transform society on Islamic principles and eventually establish an Islamic state based upon full implementation of Islamic law. In 1928 he established the Jamaat al-Ikhwan al-Muslimin (the Muslim Brotherhood) as the tool to fulfil his vision of an Islamic society in Egypt. The organization engaged in moral and social programmes such as religious education and publications, youth work, building of schools and hospitals and various other social welfare activities. Islam was perceived as an all-embracing ideology that could provide the solution to all aspects of religious, political, social and personal life. (*See also* JAMAAT-I ISLAMI)

**al-Fatiha**   *Lit. the opener.* The first SURA of the QUR'AN that is described as the essence of the revelation and is recited at least seventeen times during SALAH, the daily prayers. *Fatiha* is essential to the prayer-rite and is obligatory for the IMAM and the congregation. Bukhari, the most eminent of the HADITH collectors, stated that the Prophet had said: 'he who does not recite the *Fatiha* has not performed the prayer-rite'. In the liturgy of prayer, the *Fatiha* is always followed by AMIN repeated congregationally. In some ways, it can be compared with the *pater-noster* in Christianity. The *Fatiha* has an important role amongst Muslim mystics who have endowed it with great sanctity and believe that its repetition is an acceptable offering to God. It is also believed to have great power and can fulfil the desires of the worshipper – however, this has led to abuses of the prayer where it has been used for magical purposes. (*See also* SUFI)

**Al-hamdu-li-Llah**   *Lit. all praise belongs to Allah.* Commonly used by Muslims as an expression of thanks or gratitude to Allah.

**Ali ibn Talib**   One of the foremost of the Prophet's companions and his cousin by birth and son-in-law by marriage to Fatima. He was one of the first to accept Islam and was the father of the Prophet's grandchildren: HASAN, HUSAIN and Zainab. He became the fourth Caliph of the Muslim community after the death of UTHMAN in 656. Ali is regarded as the last of the AL-KHALIFA-UR-RASHIDUN and was known for his great piety and valour. Unfortunately his Caliphate was marred by dissent that led to several civil wars in the new community. AISHA, the youngest wife of the Prophet, sided against him and supported his rivals to the leadership. Although she was defeated and exiled in AL-MADINAH, other forces opposed him, notably the KHARIJITES and the UMAYYAD leader, MU'AWIYA. A Kharijite assassinated Ali in 661. SHI'A Muslims believe he is the rightful successor of the Prophet and the first IMAM, endowed with sinlessness and infallibility. All Muslims regard him as the epitome of nobility and chivalry. All SUFI orders (TARIQAS) except the NAQSHBANDIS believe that they originate from him.

**Alim**   Singular of ULAMA, a learned man, usually used for a religious scholar or graduate of a MADRASA.

**Alima**   The feminine equivalent of ALIM. It is unusual in traditional Islam to find women trained as religious scholars, although Muslim law does not dictate that it is not possible. There have been great women scholars in the past and some of the new Islamic revivalist movements are asserting that women should be trained as well as men. (*See also* ULAMA)

**al-Kafi**   The SHI'A collection of HADITH compiled by Muhammad ibn-Yaqub Koleini (d. 939) in the ninth century that provides the distinctive legal doctrines of the Twelver Shi'as. These *Hadith* collections provide the same functions for the Shi'a as the four collections of *Hadith* in the SUNNI tradition.

**al-Khalifa-ur-Rashidun / al-Khulafa-ur-Rashidun** *Lit. the rightly guided Caliphs.* The first four successors to the leadership of the Muslim community after the death of Muhammad; they had been amongst his early companions and his staunchest followers. After the death of ALI, the leadership of the Muslim community went to the UMAYYAD leader, MU'AWIYA, who had not been a companion. Muslims hold these first four Caliphs in high regard and believe that they kept to the right path as demonstrated by the Prophet and the Revelation contained in the QUR'AN. They are ABU BAKR, UMAR, UTHMAN and Ali.

**Allah** The One Supreme, Sovereign Creator-God who is also the same God as worshipped by the Christians and Jews. The Arabic term 'Allah' is grammatically incapable of being placed in the plural and points to the overriding urgency of the proclamation and affirmation of God's Oneness. The pre-Muslim Arabs were not unaware of the one God but they gave precedence to idols. Above all, Islam is a message to turn only to Allah for mercy and blessing and to give up all other religious allegiance to false deities. God and idolatry are incompatible. (*See also* SHIRK; TAUHID; WAHY)

**Allahu Akbar** *Lit. God is great.* Known as *takbir*, this exclamation of the supremacy of Allah is used by Muslims on numerous occasions in worship and to celebrate success or victory. It acknowledges that Allah is the source of all successful endeavour and is preferred to applause by clapping by devout Muslims. (*See also* ADHAN)

**al-Madinah / Madinah / Medina** The name given to the city of Yathrib after the Prophet migrated there from MAKKAH in 622 to, it is believed, found the first Islamic state. The invitation to come to al-Madinah arrived at a time of increasing persecution and completely changed the fortunes of the fledgling community. The date of the migration from Makkah to al-Madinah is the beginning of the Muslim calendar. In al-Madinah, the Prophet was treated with honour and regarded as the leader of al-Madinah. The city remains the second most important sacred site to the Muslim and contains the Prophet's MOSQUE and his tomb. (*See also* HIJRA)

**Amin** *Lit. so be it.* The Muslim equivalent of 'Amen' and the great utterance of the congregation at the finale of AL-FATIHA and other prayers. It is the only time that the congregants speak at the same time as the IMAM rather than following behind him.

**Amir** A traditional title that was given to a military commander, governor or prince. In religious parlance, it is used by the Muslim organization, JAMAAT-I ISLAMI, as the title for their elected leader.

**Amr** An affair or command of God. This is an important concept in that it refers to God who works and intervenes in human history. The QUR'AN acknowledges that there are incidents that would have developed differently and changed the face of human history, if God had not directly intervened. Examples would be the destruction of Sodom and Gomorrah and the saving of a remnant at the time of the flood. (*See also* AJAL)

**Anaba** *Lit. repentance.* In Islam there is no concept of original sin and although ADAM and Eve, the father and mother of the human race, committed an error before God by disobeying His injunctions, it is believed that they 'turned back' to God. This idea of turning back is central to the relationship between Allah and His creatures. The Revelation, in a sense, provides right guidance in order that repentance can take place. A prophet functions as one who asks people to turn back towards God. The penitent should return with wholeheartedness and sincerity. (*See also* DA'WA)

**Anbiya** The plural of prophet. (*See also* NABI; RASUL)

**Andhara** *Lit. to warn.* The function of all prophets is to warn human beings of the dangers of turning way from God and the rewards that come to those that turn in His direction. (*See also* NADHIR)

**Ansar** *Lit. supporters.* The term used to distinguish the Muslims of AL-MADINAH from the original followers who joined with Muhammad in MAKKAH. The Medinan Muslims accepted, helped and supported the first followers of Islam who had migrated from Makkah, escaping from the persecution of the ruling merchants of the QURAYSH. (*See also* HIJRA; MUHARJIHUN)

**Aqida**   The body of belief embodied in the QUR'AN, HADITH and four schools of law that Muslims live their lives by. With the fragmentation of the Muslim community into various movements, *aqida* has become associated with the particular interpretation maintained by distinct religious positions. (*See also* HANAFI; HANBALI; SHAFI'I; SUFI; WAHABI)

**Aql**   *Lit. reason.* There has always been a certain tension within Islam between reason denoting humanity's investigations of truth and the Revelation of God that delivers the truth. Early in Islam's history, the ASHARITES determined that theological and metaphysical issues belonged to reason, but law and ethics were under the control of the Revelation. The divide between reason and Revelation has led to some mystics and philosophers arguing the extreme position that the Revelation was for the ordinary or uneducated masses. The ULAMA closed the doors of independent use of reason to interpret Revelation in the mediaeval period however some Muslim revivalist movements have insisted that these doors remain open. In recent history influential reformers have attempted to restore the balance between reason and Revelation by asserting that they have different spheres of influence. (*See also* MUHAMMAD ABDUH; IJTIHAD; WAHY)

**Arabi, Muhiy'ud-Din ibn**   (1165–1240) Considered to be one of the greatest Muslim mystics. Born in Spain, he was a prolific writer, visionary, mystic and philosopher. His influence on the development of Sufism, the Muslim mystical tradition, is immense. He is attributed with the authorship of over six hundred books but the most widely known is the *Seals of Wisdom*. He made no secret of his contempt for the lack of spiritual understanding and general ignorance of orthodox religious scholars. (*See also* SUFI)

**Arabic**   The language in which the QUR'AN was delivered to Muhammad. As the language of the final and complete revelation from God to human beings, it is regarded as sacred. The actual words of the *Qur'an* provide a blessing over and above the meaning of the message. As they were spoken by God to the angel the words of the language of the *Qur'an* are soaked in the sacred presence of the Divine. The liturgy of prayer is also conducted in Arabic. Most Muslim children will attend classes that should minimally teach them to read the *Qur'an* even if they cannot understand it. (*See also* SALAH)

**Arafat**   A plain thirteen miles outside MAKKAH below the Mount of Mercy. On the ninth day of the HAJJ, Muslim pilgrims gather there from noon to sunset to pray and ask for forgiveness whilst some sermons are delivered. This is considered to be the culmination of the pilgrimage. Muslims believe that this is the site of the reconciliation of ADAM and Eve with God.

**Arba'in**   Collections of forty HADITH considered by the authors to be the most important or to contain the essentials of Islamic teaching. They were often decorated with wonderful calligraphy and considered to be blessed as they carried Muhammad's sayings. The number forty is also associated with patience, suffering, steadfastness and preparation, such as the forty days that Jesus spent in the desert before beginning his mission or the forty years passed by the tribes of Israel in the wilderness. Many mystics of the SUFI tradition have traditionally participated in spiritual retreats for forty days that are also known as *arba'in* or *chilla*. (*See also* SUNNA)

**Arsala**   *Lit. the message.* This refers to the message that God sends to human beings through a chosen messenger or prophet, in other words, the Revelation which lies at the heart of Islam. (*See also* RASUL; WAHY)

**Asbab an-nuzul**   *Lit. the occasions of the Revelation.* Early Muslim scholars needed to resolve the relationship between the eternality of God's final Revelation through the pre-existent QUR'AN and the fact that the individual revelations relate to specific localized events taking place in the lifetime of Muhammad. It is believed that the occasions do not undermine the universality of the *Qur'an* as God predetermines all actions and knew such events would take place from the beginning of time. The occasions were the vehicle for the revelations. (*See also* WAHY)

**Asharite**   A system of dogma that finally won over all resistance and became mainstream thought for most schools of SUNNI Islam. It was founded by Abu'l Hasan AL-ASHARI (d. 935). The Asharite view tried to resolve contradictions and argument between rationalist approaches to Revelation and tradition. (*See also* MURJI'ITE; MU'TAZILA)

**Ashraf**   The position of those who can claim ancestry to Muhammad through ALI and FATIMA. They have prestige in the Muslim world and it is felt that some of the Prophet's power to bless remains with them in a diluted form. The family name most associated with this status is Sayyid or Said. Many Muslim mystics from the SUFI tradition have claimed descent from the Prophet. In the subcontinent it is used by well-born Muslims to claim ancestry to the original Arab / Central Asian invaders and refers to someone who lives a particular lifestyle associated with high culture deriving from the court of the Mughuls. (*See also* HASAN; HUSAIN)

**Asr (salat-ul-Asr)**   The third of the five obligatory prayers to be performed by all Muslims. It is carried out either individually or communally in the MOSQUE and may be performed from late afternoon until a short while before sunset. (*See also* FAJR; ISHA; MAGHRIB; SALAH; ZUHR)

**As-Salamu-Alaykum**   *Lit. peace of God be upon you.* This is the well-known Muslim greeting. The response is *wa'alaykum salaam* (and upon you peace). The greeting of peace is also used at the completion of the prayer-rite when Muslims turn their heads to the right and then to the left, each time uttering the greeting. The greeting in the prayer-rite is offered to the two angels that accompany all human beings throughout their mortal life. However, it carries with it the connotation of greeting God, the Prophet and all believers. (*See also* SALAH)

**Awliya**   *See* WALI.

**Ayah**   A verse within a chapter of the QUR'AN. (*See also* SURA)

**Ayat**   Plural of AYAH.

**Ayatollah**  *Lit. sign of God.* The highest rank of SHI'A religious scholar and cleric. It is believed that certain scholars are of high enough rank to carry out IJTIHAD, or personal interpretation of the Revelation. Amongst these scholars there are those who are believed to be in spiritual contact with the Hidden IMAM and therefore his agents or viceroys on earth. These are known as *ayatollahs* and are able to interpret the mind of the Hidden Imam. At various times in history there has been one *ayatollah* who has risen above all others to become the leader of the Shi'a community. (*See also* KHOMEINI)

**Aza'im**  The art of exorcism of evil spirits or JINN. Aza'im probably derives from *al-azm*, resoluteness of opinion, and is a command to others that is obligatory to obey. Thus the exorcist, through the power that God invests in him, is able to command *jinn* and other demons. (*See also* SIHR)

**Azraqites**  One of the sects of KHARIJITES that developed shortly after the death of Muhammad. All the Kharijite groups believed that the leadership of the Muslims should be invested in the community and that leaders should be elected and removed by majority opinion. The Azraqites believed that it was not sufficient to merely hold to correct belief but that it was also a mark of disbelief to remain at home and not join them in active JIHAD. Such disbelief was punishable by death.

**B**

**Badr**   A battle fought by Muhammad and the first Muslims in March 624 CE. Three hundred Muslims defeated a much larger force of Meccans. This victory following close on Muhammad's new position of leadership in AL-MADINA provided the impetus for a theological change to take place. The doctrine of 'Manifest Success' which links divine approval to worldly success became the norm for SUNNI Muslims. This established a pattern of religious revival being linked to social, political or economic failure as Muslims responded to decline as a mark of Allah's disapproval. (*See also* UHUD)

**Bai'a / Bai'at**   The traditional oath of allegiance made to a SHAIKH on commencing discipleship or joining a TARIQA. A traditional *bai'at* might consist of a reaffirmation of the SHAHADAH. In the subcontinent, some *bai'ats* involve the new disciple holding one end of an unraveled turban whilst the Shaikh holds the other, imitating a wedding ceremony and demonstrating the importance of the Shaikh / MURID (master / disciple relationship). The new disciple is initiated into the level of practice suitable to his / her stage of awareness. (*See also* SUFI)

**Bait al-Mal / Bait ul-Mal**   *Lit. house of wealth.* A term used for the public treasury in Muslim nations or for the post of treasurer in some Muslim organizations.

**Balkafiyya**   Those who maintain the position of BI-LA KAYF.

**Barah wafat**   The twelfth night of the third lunar month, *Rabi' al-awwal*, which is remembered as both the day of Muhammad's birth and the night of his death. It is major celebration throughout the Muslim world but is better known as MAULID. Indian Muslims still acknowledge the night of Muhammad's death on this day of general festivity by spending the night in the MOSQUE praying and listening to sermons.

**Baraka / Barakat**   *Lit. blessing.* This has to be understood as a special power that radiates from certain objects, holy men and women and, of course, the words of the QUR'AN as they are in touch with the hidden or mystical power of the divine world. Many Muslims and SUFIS believe the power to bless is inherent in a saint, his tomb and his relics. It also applies to anything that has belonged to Muhammad. Baraka is usually received through physical contact but it is also existent in the *Qur'an* and the words of the Revelation. (*See also* SHAIKH)

**Barelwi**   A nineteenth-century movement founded by Ahmed Riza Khan Barelwi in order to counter the criticisms originating from DEOBAND and other reform movements. The Barelwis did not desire to change religious practice, but adhered to custom-laden styles of Sufism and closely allied themselves to the teachings of the mediaeval PIRS. They defended vigorously any custom that raised the status of Muhammad and the saints. (*See also* AHL AL-SUNNA WA JAMAAT; AWLIYA; SUFI)

**Barzakh**   The term used to define the role of Muhammad as the intermediary between the creation and the Divine world. Ibn ARABI, the great SUFI teacher, elaborated a theosophy in which Muhammad becomes the manifesting principle of the Divine and the bridge between the numinon and the phenomenon. The term is also applied to other kinds of intermediary worlds between this one and the next such as the stay in the grave until the Day of Judgment (*See also* BHIDHR; NUR I MUHAMMADI).

**Bashar**   *Lit. a human being.* In Islam, human beings are created from clay, enthused with the spirit of God and given the privilege of being

17

God's KHALIFA or representative on earth. The central role of all human beings is submission to the sovereignty of Allah and therefore God selects chosen human beings as His messengers and recipients of revelation. This closeness to Allah resulted in the angels being asked to prostrate before the first human, ADAM. IBLIS refused out of pride, as he is created from fire not clay, and was expelled to become the tempter of human beings.

**Basmalla / Bismillah**  *See* BISMILLAH-IR-RAHMAN-IR-RAHIM.

**Basri, Hasan al-**  (d. 728) Regarded as the epitome of Medinan piety and asceticism in the early years of the UMAYYAD empire. He opposed the doctrine of predestination and argued that human beings are responsible for their own actions. Many SUFI orders (TARIQA) include him as an early member of their chains of masters that go back to the Prophet. He is regarded as one of the great forerunners of the mystical tradition. (*See also* SILSILA)

**Bektashi**  A SUFI order (TARIQA) founded by Hajji Bektash of Khurusan (d. 1338) that is strongly influenced by SHI'A. The order was extremely successful in Anatolia and spread down into the Balkans. In its heyday under the OTTOMAN sultans, it became a kind of guild for the Janisseries – the special elite chosen by the ruler from amongst Christians in order to ensure personal loyalty. The Bektashis have therefore also been influenced by Christian doctrines and practice.

**Be-pir (Urdu)**  *Lit. without a pir / Shaikh.* An expression used to describe someone who is cruel or heartless. The link of a heartless person to an individual who is without the guidance of SHAIKH or spiritual master indicates the importance of the SUFI tradition of personal guidance in the subcontinental forms of Islam. (*See also* MURID)

**Bhidhr**  *Lit. seed.* The mystical conception that Muhammad pre-existed ADAM as first creation of God and is therefore the archetypal perfect man or seed of the human race. This theosophy is depicted in songs and poetry throughout the Muslim world. (*See also* BARZAKH; NUR I MUHAMMADI; SUFI)

**Bid'a**   An illegal innovation in religion. In a religion that is based on Revelation of divine law and maintains a central relationship to God through obedience, it is important to know what is permissible or correct. Islam has developed a sophisticated approach to defining correct practice and belief throughout its history, but many sects and movements have developed their own interpretation or modification of that practice. The issue of *bid'a* therefore becomes a thorny debate between scholars as to whether a particular innovation is legal or illegal. All parties will attempt to defend their position from tradition. (*See also* HADITH; IJMA; IJTIHAD, QIYAS)

**Bi-la kayf**   *Lit. without how.* The doctrine that deals with the anthropomorphic passages in the QUR'AN such as 'the hand of God', 'the face of God' or 'the throne of God'. Since anthropomorphism presented the believer with an intellectual challenge to Islam's uncompromising monotheism, one solution was to take these passages as belonging to God's own understanding of His nature and not try to investigate the meaning either literally or metaphorically. This is still a current debate between SALAFI and WAHABI movements who maintain the above position and traditional Muslims who maintain that metaphorical interpretation is permissible (*See also* SALAFI; SUFI; TAUHID; WAHHABI).

**Bilal**   (d. 641) A black Ethiopian companion of Muhammad who tradition asserts was the first MU'ADHIN appointed by the Prophet to call the prayer. Bilal had adopted Islam very early in the career of Muhammad, whilst still a slave. He had been tortured by his owner because of his allegiance to the new faith and was purchased from slavery by ABU BAKR. In popular tradition he has become the symbol of black people who have embraced Islam and is regarded as the exemplar of Islam's creed to know no differentiation of races. Contemporary black Muslim movements acknowledge him as a kind of patron saint and some have even adopted the term 'Bilalian' to describe themselves. (*See also* ADHAN)

**Bismillah-ir-Rahman-ir-Rahim**   *Lit. in the name of Allah, the all-gracious and all-merciful.* Known as the *Basmalla*, it is the preface to all the

SURAS of the QUR'AN except for the ninth. Unlike the Jews who decided that the Name of God was too sacred to be uttered, Muslims sanctify all activities by its repetition. It is usually recited before eating food or commencing any action such as entering a room or a premises; opening a book; before drinking; after yawning; or entering bed. The formula is traditionally included at the beginning of a book and many Muslims will not read a text where it is not included. The sacred formula contains BARAKA, a blessing, and can be used to ward off evil or misfortune or protect against the supernatural. (*See also* DHIKR)

**Bistami, Abu Yazid** (d. 874) A well-known SUFI mystic who is attributed with being the first to express the idea of FANA or annihilation of the lower self and absorption into the Divine Attributes. Bistami is accredited with uttering various statements when ecstatic which seem to indicate complete unity between himself and Allah. These were explained as divine intoxication and the person was not held responsible as not considered to be in a normal state of consciousness.

**Bukhari, Muhammad ibn Ishmael al-** (810–70) The most authoritative collector of HADITH whose collection is known as the greatest authority in Islam after the QUR'AN. During the ninth century various scholars took on the massive task of travelling the Muslim world to collect together the sayings and deeds of the Prophet. By this time there were many spurious ones that needed to be sifted out. Al-Bukhari was particularly strict and reduced hundreds of thousands to only a few thousand. (*See also* SAHIH MUSLIM)

**Buraq** The heavenly steed brought by an angel to Muhammad to take him on his mystical night journey. It is described by poets as being smaller than a horse with a woman's head and a peacock tail. Its depiction is regarded as giving protection to believers and it is possible to find wonderful paintings of Buraq on trucks in Pakistan and Afghanistan. There is also a genre of miniature paintings that depict the mythical creature. (*See also* MI'RAJ)

**Burda** *See* KHIRQA-I SHARIF.

**Burqa**    The veil worn by women in order to conform to the insistence of the QUR'AN's dress codes regarding modesty for both men and women. The *burqa* is usually associated with the strictest kind of veiling where a cloak is worn over the clothes and covers the head, body and legs. Often there is only a slit for the eyes. (*See also* HIJAB)

**Caliph**   *See* KHALIFA.

**Chilla**   *See* ARBA'IN.

**Chishti / Chishtiya / Chishtiyya**   The largest SUFI order or TARIQA in the subcontinent, founded by Mu'inuddin Chishti of Ajmer (d. 1236) also known as Hazrat Gharib Nawaz (the Helper of the Poor). The Sufis of the Chishti order are famous for their use of QAWWALIS – ecstatic music sung in devotion to Allah. The Chishtis are sometimes accused of adopting Hindu practices and there is no doubt that the latter have influenced more eclectic forms of universal Sufism through such teachers as Hazrat Inayat Khan who taught in Europe and the USA in the first half of the twentieth century. The shrine centre at Ajmer where Mu'inuddin Chishti lived and was buried is famous throughout India and is visited by millions of pilgrims that include Hindus and Sikhs. (*See also* MU'INUDDIN CHISHTI)

**Chishti, Mu'inuddin**   (1142–1236) The historical founder of the CHISHTI TARIQA that is very popular in the Indian subcontinent. Mu'inuddin Chishti studied the traditional Islamic subjects of QUR'AN and HADITH in central Asia but was not satisfied and began to pursue a spiritual quest that took him into discipleship under Khwaja Uthman Herwani, a Chishti master from Persia. Mu'inuddin Chishti travelled and studied with his master for over twenty years but after a visit to MAKKAH and AL-MADINHA he received instructions to promote Islam in India. After a forty-day retreat at the tomb of Shaikh Hujwiri in Lahore, he made his way to Ajmer in Rajasthan. He lived a very pious and simple life and quickly began to attract converts and disciples. It is said that he personally brought 40,000 families into the fold of Islam. Today, his shrine is one of the most famous in all India.

**Dala'il** *Lit. proofs.* A form of literature that praises Muhammad. The *dala'il* collections are essentially biographies that are complemented by miracle stories. They detail Muhammad's genealogy and noble qualities and contain a variety of miracle stories whereby men and women were able to recognize his special status as God's final messenger. Famous collections were composed by Abu Nu'aim al-Isfahani (d. 1037) and al-Baihaqi (d. 1066). (*See also* SIRA)

**Dar / Dargah** A shrine to a Muslim holy man and a place of pilgrimage. Often the *dargahs* are the place where a SUFI or pious man spent his life in remembrance of Allah and teaching. After death, the tomb becomes a place of veneration. Pilgrims will come to receive the saint's blessings and use him for prayers of intercession. The poor and the destitute are usually allowed to stay in the *dargah* for periods of time and some may manage communal kitchens to feed the poor and travellers. Generally, there is an attached MOSQUE for worship and special gatherings will take place for DHIKR (the remembrance of God). The place may remain a centre of teaching under the direction of the Sufi's spiritual descendents. (*See also* MAZAR; TARIQA)

**Dar al-Amn** *Lit. abode of peace.* Used to describe territory that is not under Islamic law but where Muslims can live in peace and harmony without interference in their practice of Islam. (*See also* DAR AL-HARB, DAR AL-ISLAM)

**Dar al-Harb**    *Lit. abode of war.* Territory that is not under the juris-diction of Islamic law or geographical areas that are not under the control of Islam. The distinction of *dar al-Harb* and *dar al-Islam* has been crucial in Muslim thought and action. *Dar al-Harb* remains territory that can be brought into submission to God's will by active proselytising, or if threatening to the *dar al-Islam*, can be overcome by JIHAD. (*See also* DA'WA)

**Dar al-Islam**    *Lit. abode of Islam.* Territory that is under Islamic law or the geographical domain of Muslim faith and practice. In spite of the encroachment of national loyalties there is still a strong sense of an overriding Muslim identity or membership of the UMMA (community), and Islam remains a religion committed to bringing the world under the dominion of Allah. (*See also* DAR AL-HARB; DA'WA; JIHAD)

**Dar al-ulum / Dar al-uloom / Dar ul-ulum**    *Lit. a bode of sciences.* Higher institutions for the study of Islamic religious education. (*See also* MADRASA)

**Darban (Urdu)**    The doorkeeper who guards the entrance to a shrine, protects the sacred space from unwelcome intrusion, and maintains some control on the influx of devotees waiting to enter. (*See also* DAR; MAZAR)

**Dars i Nizami**    An Islamic curriculum devised by Farangi Mahal, a college in Lucknow during the eighteenth century that still forms the basis for religious education in the MADRASAS of the subcontinent. The curriculum was divided into two parts: MANQULAT, which consisted of the study of QUR'AN and HADITH, and MA'QULAT which consisted of the study of law, logic and philosophy. The emphasis was originally on the latter but most modern *madrasas* have placed *manqulat* at the centre of the curriculum and many will not teach philosophy.

**Da'wa / Da'wah**    *Lit. call.* The promotion of Islam to both Muslims and non-Muslims that is considered to be a central duty for all Muslims. *Da'wa* may be achieved either by preaching or exemplary good actions. The majority of twentieth-century *da'wa* movements are engaged in preaching activities inside the Muslim community trying to bring back lapsed Muslims to the practice of their faith. However, Islam remains a proselytizing religion and attracts converts wherever it is established. In the twentieth century there has been a huge increase in the use of tracts, leaflets and pamphlets to promote various aspects of the religion. (*See also* TABLIGH-I JAMAAT)

**Dawud**  The Muslim name for David, believed to be the Prophet of Allah to whom the Book of Psalms (ZABUR) was revealed. (*See also* NABI; RASUL)

**Deoband**  A famous Muslim college founded in 1867 in Northern India in a small town of the same name. The founders had all fought against the British in 1857 and realized that there was no longer any hope of defeating the invader by a call to JIHAD. Their vision was to maintain the integrity of Muslim belief and practice through education and to close the ranks of the community upon itself for protection from the non-Muslim population. The aim of the founders was to train ULAMA who would be committed to a conservative reform of Islam based on their interpretation of HADITH. The school went on to become a powerful and influential reform movement, essentially anti-mystic but without the political dimension of the twentieth-century revivalist movements. It remains influential throughout the subcontinent and wherever subcontinental Muslims have established migrant communities. There are around 10,000 Deobandi colleges in the subcontinent. (*See also* BARELWI; TABLIGH-I JAMAAT)

**Dhajjal, al-**  The antichrist figure who in Muslim eschatological traditions will appear on the earth just prior to the return of ISA (Jesus) and the MAHDI, when he will be overthrown by Isa, and the world will embrace the religion of God before the final Day of Judgment.

**Dhikr / Zhikr**  The essential message of the QUR'AN to remember Allah. Although the *Qur'an* extols prayer as a central means of remembrance it praises those who remember Allah in all walks and arenas of life. Consequently, the SUFI mystics developed methods to remember

Allah at all times. The most common is the distinctive repetitive and rhythmic recollection of the names of Allah in various formulas. Each Sufi TARIQA has its own unique form of *dhikr* as practised by its great exponents and believed to date back to the founder of the order. A MURID (follower) will be initiated into both individual and communal *dhikr* on initiation into the order. The most common form of *dhikr* is the repetition of LA' ILAHA ILLA ALLAH, the first clause of the SHAHADAH, either aloud or in silence. *Dhikr* is also used to describe reading sections of the *Qur'an* or remembering Allah in the heart. (*See also* SHAIKH)

**Dhikra**    One of the main activities of a prophet of God to remind the people to remember Allah and offer submission to the One true God. *Dhikra* goes alongside the prophet's instruction to warn of the penalties of disobedience. (*See also* ARSALA; NABI; NADHIR; RASUL)

**Dhimmi / Zimmi**    Non-Muslims belonging to one of the revealed religions, such as Christians and Jews who live in Muslim territory and therefore have protected status as People of the Book. They are subject to a special tax in lieu of ZAKAH. (*See also* AHL AL-KITAB)

**Dhul-Hijjah**    The last month of the Muslim lunar calendar and the time of the pilgrimage to MAKKAH known as the HAJJ.

**Dhu'l-nun**    (796–861) Born in Upper Egypt and an extensive traveller in Syria and Arabia, Dhu'l-nun was an influential SUFI mystic who was one of the first to talk about a mystical union based on the relationship of lover and Beloved. Before conversion to Islam he was an alchemist and there is some speculation that he was influenced by Egyptian Hermeticism. He was arrested in 829 in Baghdad for heresy but was released on the Caliph's orders to return to Cairo. His tombstone remains in the city and is a site of veneration.

**Din / Deen**    *Lit. a way of life.* The Arabic term used for religion and its practices, although it conveys far more than the usual Western concept of religion. It is used to convey the idea of a primordial religion that exists within God and appears to human beings as an unchanging or eternal Revelation. Individual revealed religions are expressions of the *din*. The core or essence will remain the same but there will be unique expressions according to time and culture. Islam is the final *din* and closest to the primordial *din*. The term conveys the idea that religion is all-encompassing and influences every aspect of human life right down to everyday details of human existence. *Din* is not confined to private individual devotion but is an overarching, all-comprehensive view which permeates the whole of society. (*See also* DIN AL-FITRAH; FITRAH; WAHY)

**Din al-Fitrah**    A term used to describe Islam as the natural way of life for all human beings to live. It is founded on the idea that there is a natural religion or way of life which is innate to human nature before contact with society. All the world's religions are believed to have arisen from contact with this innate capacity for righteousness but Islam is the ideal expression of FITRAH. (*See also* DIN)

**Djinn**    *See* JINN.

**Du'a**    Free prayer as opposed to the five daily ritual prayers that are obligatory for all Muslims. *Du'a* consists of varying forms of personal prayer often containing supplication and pleading for intercession, sometimes made through Muhammad. *Du'a* prayers do not follow any necessary pattern or ritual and the petitioners may use their own words, derivations from the QUR'AN or other sources. (*See also* SALAH)

**Durud-i Sharif**    Popular prayers that bless Muhammad, the Prophet of God. These are often sung by the faithful in beautiful tunes. The praises and blessing of the Prophet were introduced throughout the Muslim world by travelling SUFIS who highly venerated the Prophet. (*See also* BHIDR; MUHAMMAD)

# E

**Eid**   *See* ID.

**Eid al-Adha**   *See* IL AL-ADHA.

**Eid al-Fitr**   *See* ID AL-FITR.

**Eid Mubarak / Id Mubarak**   A greeting and a blessing exchanged between Muslims at the two festivals of ID. (*See also* ID UL-ADHA; ID UL-FITR)

**Fajr (Salat-ul-Fajr)**   The first of the five daily obligatory prayers, or dawn prayer, which can be performed from dawn until just before sunrise. (*See also* SALAH; RAK'AH)

**Fakir**   *See* FAQIR.

**Falah**   The Muslim prayer-call summons the faithful not only to SALAH (prayer) but also to *falah* (the good). This central concept of Islam moves the religion away from personal piety to a communal thrust built on social welfare and prosperity. Islam is fulfilled in this social order in which well-being can be achieved in the Muslim environment. Religion is thus about behaviour as well as belief and individual piety. (*See also* ADHAN; UMMA)

**Falasifa**   Muslims who became interested in Greek thought and utilized philosophy to develop, substantiate and modify orthodox Islamic doctrine. This led to the development of KALAM, or Muslim theology. From 800–1100, many Muslim thinkers adopted Greek ideas, particularly neo-Platonism, but the Falasifa movement went into decline after the challenge from GHAZALI (d. 1111). Greek thought survived but only if it was completely assimilated or submerged into Muslim doctrine.

**Fana**   A term used in Sufism to describe the complete loss of self or annihilation caused by the experience of the unity of Allah. In some SUFI traditions there is a progression of degrees of *fana*, beginning with annihilation of the self through complete identity with the SHAIKH. However, as the *Shaikh* is believed to have submerged his own identity into the Prophet Muhammad, he will lead the MURID (disciple) towards *fana f'ir rasul* (annihilation into the Prophet). The Prophet will then lead the *murid* to the final annihilation into Allah. (*See also* ADAB)

**Faqir (Urdu) / Fakir**  A wandering SUFI mendicant who lives only for God in a vow of poverty. (*See also* QALANDARI)

**Fard**  One of the five categories of Islamic law. It is an obligatory duty imposed by the Revelation which is punished by God if omitted – for example, the five pillars of Islam. (*See also* HALAL; HARAM; SHARA)

**Fatamids**  A Muslim dynasty that began in Tunisia but took control of Egypt where they founded the city of Cairo. The name derives from the belief that they descended from FATIMAH, the daughter of the Prophet, and her husband (the fourth Caliph). As followers of the murdered fourth Caliph, the Fatamids were SHI'ITES of the ISHMAELI or Seveners tradition. Their religious rivals were the orthodox Sunni and Abbasid Caliphs. The Fatamids under al-Mo'izz conquered Egypt from North Africa in 969 and remained there in varying states of rule to 1171. At the peak of their power, the Fatamids ruled much of North Africa and Syria as far north as Mosul. During their rule of Egypt they founded the university of AL-AZHAR, which eventually became a Sunni establishment and the most authoritative institution in the Muslim world.

**Fatihah / Fatiha**  See AL-FATIHA.

**Fatima (al-Zahrah)**  Known as *al-Zahrah* (the luminous). The only one of Muhammad's four daughters to outlive him. She was married to ALI and was the mother of HASAN, HUSAIN and Zainab, the grandchildren of the Prophet. She is a legendary figure who is surrounded by miracle stories. She is highly respected in SHI'A as the mother of the Prophet's bloodline. It is said that light surrounded her birth and that she never menstruated. She was honoured with the title of 'virgin'. In Shi'a tradition Muhammad, Ali, Fatima, and their two sons are known as the Panjtan (the Five People). It is said that Muhammad took them under his cloak to show their unity with him. (*See also* AHL AL-BAIT)

**Fatwa**    The legal opinion or religious decision made by a Muslim scholar on the basis of an interpretation required to demonstrate correct observance in novel situations. It is the application of the SHARI'A (Islamic law) to a particular case or situation so that it may be used as a precedent. A *fatwa* may be issued by a member of the ULAMA but may be contradicted by the scholars of a different tradition within the religion. There is no central authority for issuing a *fatwa*. (*See also* IJMA; IJTIHAD; QIYAS)

**Fiqh**    *Lit. understanding.* The personal understanding of a scholar organized into a disciplined body of knowledge achieved by deduction. This personal activity developed into a structured discipline of Islamic jurisprudence utilizing Islamic methodology. It comprises the legal order of Islam according to the four authoritative schools of law in the SUNNI tradition and one in the SHI'A tradition. Decisions concerning new events that require a legal ruling are usually taken from the body of *fiqh* rather than direct from the scriptural source. *Fiqh* has traditionally been the preserve of the ULAMA but recent twentieth-century revivalist movements have sometimes insisted that the corpus of *fiqh* can be ignored and scholars can go direct to QUR'AN and HADITH for clarity and understanding. (*See also* HANAFI; HANBALI; IJMA; IJTIHAD; MALIKI; QIYAS; SHAFI'I)

**Firasa**    A type of mystical intuition or wisdom possessed by Muslim saints or SUFIS which allowed the individual to see into the innermost character or thoughts of another person, in particular, where the character can impact on the future events in a person's life. Firasa is also used to describe a form of divination where physiognomy could be used to decode the inner character by observing physical features.

**Fitna / Fitnah**    A term originally used to describe the persecution suffered by Muslims in the name of religion but later used for sedition or conspiracy against an Islamic state.

**Fitrah**  The idea of an innate nature which contains a blueprint of the original form of the divine law. For this reason a human being may be propelled towards God and the good even without the aid of revelation. Because of *fitrah* it is believed that every child is born into natural Islam or submission to God. However, without the aid of Revelation, *fitrah* is overcome by social conditioning and the temptations of SHAITAN. In the mystical tradition, a person should follow their heart as it will lead them towards God since the heart is perceived to be the seat of *fitrah*. Islam is believed to be the religion most closely corresponding to *fitrah*. (*See also* DIN AL-FITRAH)

**Furqan, al-**  A name for the QUR'AN that refers to its function of providing correct guidance as the source of discrimination between truth and falsehood for believers.

# G

**Gharib al-Hadith** The study of the HADITH in order to ascertain the meaning of difficult words based on their linguistic origin. The most famous work is that of the twelfth-century scholar, al-Zamakshari.

**Ghazali, Ahmad al-** (d. 1111) Arguably the greatest of all Muslim scholars and said to be the best Muslim after the Prophet. As a theologian and a mystic, al-Ghazali succeeded in refuting the ideas of Muslim philosophers who had borrowed heavily from Greek thought, but he also resolved the tensions between orthodoxy and Sufism by bringing the two closer together. In order to do this he challenged extreme mystical claims of union, incarnation and absorption by asserting that God could only be related to or known to the degree that He chose to reveal Himself to human beings. This Revelation is contained in the Divine Names which can be penetrated through mysticism. Ghazali's own journey was that of a spiritual seeker. He had originally rejected orthodox Muslim theology on the grounds that it was too formalistic and exoteric. However, after a thorough study of Greek philosophy, that too was rejected as being far from Islamic thought and providing no grounds for certainty. He finally concluded that certainty could only be found in the experiential dimension of Sufism but that Islamic mysticism had to be rooted in the *Qur'anic* revelation. (*See also* FALASIFA; KALAM; SUFI)

**Ghusl** The formal washing of the complete body prior to worship, or the greater ablution. It is required in certain circumstances such as sexual activity before the prayer, when the normal WUDU is not sufficient.

**Giarvin Sharif**   The celebration of SUFI teachings that usually takes place on a Thursday evening amongst the followers of a Sufi order and is often associated with Abdul Qadir GILANI, the founder of the QADIRIYA TARIQA. The event will take place after the evening prayer and consists of DHIKR, DU'A and blessings given to Muhammad and well-known Sufis.

**Gilani, Abdul Qadir**   The founder of the QADIRIYA SUFI order (TARIQA) but considered to be the archetypal Sufi and the *al-Qutb al-Azam* – the summit of sainthood and the spiritual ruler of the world, the perfect man who inherits the spiritual perfection of Muhammad. As such he is acknowledged by all the Sufi orders and many of them maintain Thursday night as a time of worship in his honour. He was born in 1077 in Iran and went to study in Baghdad. After a long period of retreat in the desert he began to preach in the city. The vast amount of hagiographical material concerning miracle stories makes it very difficult to establish Gilani's biography with any accuracy but there is no doubt of the veneration with which he is received by pious traditional Muslims throughout the Islamic world. (*See also* QUTB)

**Hadhrat / Hazrat (Urdu)**   *Lit. dignity, nearness*. A title given to an eminent SUFI or a Companion of Muhammad. It is very often used in the subcontinental CHISHTI TARIQA as a title for the SHAIKHS of the order.

**Hadith**   The extensive collections of sayings attributed to Muhammad that form the second most authoritative scriptural source for Muslim belief and practice after the QUR'AN. They are different from the *Qur'an* in that they were inspired by Muhammad's own initiative rather than by Allah. In the eighth and ninth century, various scholars began the process of collecting and collating the *Hadith* from all over the Muslim world on the basis of their reliability. Six collections came to be regarded as reliable and authoritative. The two most eminent are BUKHARI and Muslim. Although some Western scholars have challenged the view that the *Hadith* genuinely represent the views and actions of the Prophet, Muslim scholars use them as the secondary source for establishing precedent based on the SUNNA of the Prophet. Each *hadith* is divided into parts, ISNAD and *matn*. Whereas *matn* provides the main body of text of the *Hadith* itself, it is *isnad* that demonstrates the degree of reliability. (*See also* HADITH QUDSI)

**Hadith Qudsi**   A special kind of HADITH that are believed to have been voiced by Muhammad but whose meaning and content were inspired by Allah. Any *hadith*, which has been deemed to be *Hadith al-Qudsi* is regarded as more authoritative and accepted by most Muslims.

**Hafiz**   A person who has learnt to recite the complete QUR'AN by memory. It has always been an important concern of Muslims that the *Qur'an* should be passed on without error orally as well as in written form. Most children are taught recitation of the *Qur'an* from an early age and some go on to complete the full *Qur'an*. Hafiz have a special status in the community and are also called upon to provide recitations on religious or civil occasions. (*See also* MADRASA)

**Hajar**   The wife of the Prophet IBRAHIM (Abraham) and mother of the Prophet ISHMAEL. According to the Islamic view of history, Hajar and her son were cast out because of the jealousy of Abraham's first wife, Sara. They wandered in the desert until coming to the area where MAKKAH is now situated. They were both dying of thirst but through a miracle water sprung forth from the ground underneath the feet of the small child. The pair remained in this place and were visited by Ibrahim who built the altar known as the KA'ABA for the worship of the one God. (*See also* KA'BAH; ZAMZAM)

**Hajj**   The annual pilgrimage to MAKKAH and the fifth of the five pillars of Islam. It is a religious duty for every Muslim to complete at least once in their life if they are in good health and can afford to go. However, it is possible to have the *Hajj* undertaken on your behalf by proxy. Muslims who have completed the *Hajj* are entitled to be called *Hajji* (male) and *Hajjah* (female). The pilgrimage takes place in the month of *Dhu'l-Hijjah* and before departure the pilgrim enters a consecrated state symbolized by wearing a simple cotton cloth thrown across the body leaving one shoulder and arm bare. It is forbidden to shave or wash apart from ritual ablutions performed at various stages of the pilgrimage. Sexual relations are also forbidden. On arrival in Makkah, the pilgrim first makes seven circumambulations of the KA'ABA and if possible kisses the Black Stone in the wall of the shrine. After this, the pilgrim runs back and forth between two small hills just outside the MOSQUE. This commemorates HAJAR's desperate search for water. After listening to preaching in the mosque, the pilgrim sets out for MINA and ARAFAT. On the ninth day, the pilgrim stands in the sun from noon to sunset in Mina, five miles from Makkah in the desert, and listens to sermons. On the following day, there is the ritual stoning of SHAITAN which symbolizes the victory of IBRAHIM when the devil tempted him to disobey God's command to sacrifice ISHMAEL. After the stoning a sheep is sacrificed and the pilgrims shave their heads. The pilgrims then return to Makkah where they circumambulate the *Ka'aba* again and then pass three days in rest and relaxation. After a farewell visit to the Great Mosque, the pilgrims return home.

**Halal**  A term used to describe any action which is permitted or lawful for a Muslim, and that does not contradict the laws of God. It is more often used for Muslim dietary laws concerning the slaughter of permitted animals in such a way as to drain them of blood. The QUR'AN also forbids the eating of pig, carrion, birds of prey, blood, animals that died of sickness or through being killed by a carnivore or were slaughtered as sacrifice to an idol. (*See also* HARAM)

**Hallaj, Mansur al-**  (858–922) A famous mystic from Persia who was murdered by the orthodox for uttering 'ana'l Haqq' (I am the Truth). Al-Hallaj had been a follower of several prominent SUFIS and his own poetry resounds with ecstatic and intoxicated divine love. Amongst contemporary Sufis, his reputation is untarnished and he is considered one of the greatest amongst the lovers of God. However, it is acknowledged that he may have gone too far in his expression of his intoxication. (*See also* FANA)

**Hamd**  Thankful praise of Allah expressed through various phrases in Arabic, the most common being HAMDU LILLAH. A devout Muslim would try to thank God even in situations of distress or crisis. The QUR'AN states: *if you give thanks, I will give you increase* (14:7). Gratitude is believed to bring with it spiritual joy and it may be that absence of gratitude will run the risk of loss of grace. This uttering of thankful praise is a solitary activity unlike the obligatory SALAH. (*See also* DU'A)

**Hamdu lillah**  *Lit. praise be to God.* The first line of the first SURA of the QUR'AN and the most commonly repeated thankful praise of Allah expressed by Muslims. (*See also* HAMD)

**Hanafi**  A school of Islamic jurisprudence founded by ABU HANIFA (d. 767) in Baghdad. Although the largest school of law in the Muslim world, it is the dominant school in Western Asia, lower Egypt and the subcontinent. (*See also* FIQH; HANBALI; MADHAB; MALIKI; SHAFI'I)

**Hanbali**  One of the four schools of SUNNI Islamic jurisprudence founded by Ahmad Ibn Hanbal (d. 855). Ibn Hanbal was a traditionalist who supported the use of HADITH to create Islamic law. He had opposed the rationalist views of the MU'TAZILITES and passed a period in prison for refusing to acknowledge that that the QUR'AN was not eternal. His teachings were organized by his followers after his death into one of the four schools of law. It is the dominant school in Northern and Central Asia but its teachings were revived by the eighteenth-century WAHABI movement in Arabia. (*See also* HANAFI; MALIKI; SHAFI'I; SHARI'A)

**Hanif**  A God-seeker. Islam recognizes that there were pious, faithful worshippers of the one God prior to its advent, even outside the ranks of Jews and Christians. These monotheists, who before the coming of Islam maintained monotheism amongst the pagan Arab tribes, are generally ascribed the title of *Hanif*. Usually they are associated with various individuals who tried to maintain the worship of one God at the KA'ABA stone in MAKKAH and opposed the installation of idols at the shrine.

**Haqiqa**  The inner reality or the Truth where the presence of God is found in the human heart after inner purification. In Sufism, *haqiqat* becomes the goal, but most SUFIS have acknowledged that *haqiqa* (the internal reality) and SHARI'A (the external law) should accompany the ideal Muslim life. Sufism has developed extensive practices for the purification of the ego (NAFS) so that the state of *haqiqat* can be revealed or discovered. These mostly consist of the remembrance (DHIKR) of Allah's divine names. (*See also* HAQQ)

**Haqiqa Muhammadiya**  The way of imitation of the Prophet Muhammad much loved by the practitioners of Muslim mysticism, the SUFIS. Muhammad is regarded as both the exemplar of the Muslim revelation and the primal mystic who is fully surrendered to the will of Allah. Practitioners of the Sufi path attempt to model themselves on the Prophet's example and even physical appearance. The intention is to arrive at his spiritual relationship of surrender but not to imitate his relationship of prophethood. (*See also* ADAB; MUHAMMAD; SHAIKH; TARIQA)

**Haqq**   *Lit. the Truth*. The Divine Reality that is behind and within all created phenomenon. It is one of the ninety-nine Names or Attributes of Allah and used by SUFIS in their recitation. It is Allah's presence as Truth that allows the mystic to discover reality as an indwelling presence found in the purified heart. (*See also* HAQIQA; QALB)

**Haram**   The fifth of the five categories of action that constitute the SHARI'A (Islamic law). *Haram* refers to actions which are unlawful or forbidden and are definitely punished if performed. The general principle of Islam is that all things are deemed to be lawful unless expressly prohibited in the QUR'AN. It is therefore God who has decreed what is forbidden in His Revelation rather than the decisions of human executive bodies or governments. (*See also* FARD; MAKRUH; MANDUB; MUBAH)

**Haram Sharif**   The grand MOSQUE in MAKKAH that contains the KA'ABA, the well of ZAMZAM and the hills of MARWAH and SAFA. It is the foremost mosque in the Islamic world and the centre of the rites that take place on the annual pilgrimage. (*See also* HAJJ; ZAMZAM)

**Hasan**   The grandson of Muhammad, son of ALI and FATIMA and brother of HUSAIN. He is regarded by SHI'A Muslims as the second IMAM and the third rightful leader of the Muslim community. The Shi'a believe that when MU'AWIYYA achieved the leadership of the Muslim community and established the UMAYYAD dynasty, he promised that on his death he would return the leadership of the community to Ali's children, HASAN and Husain. It is believed that Mu'awiyya paid Hasan a bribe to live in AL-MADINAH and not attempt to establish his claim. He died in mysterious circumstances in al-Madinah and Shi'a Muslims believe that he was poisoned on Mu'awiyya's instructions. (*See also* KARBALA)

**Hawa** The enemy within described in the QUR'AN as the 'self urgent to evil' (12:53). This inclination to waywardness arising out of human imperfection or weakness has to be fought against and mastered. The directions of the *Qur'an* and the life of Muhammad provide the two great inspirations and guides for self-mastery and submission to God. (*See also* DHIKR; NAFS)

**Hidaya / Hidayah** A legal textbook brought to India by MAULANA Buhari-uddin from Central Asia in the thirteenth century. It has remained the basis for Muslim law in the subcontinent.

**Hifz** The traditional method of learning to recite the QUR'AN in Arabic. (*See also* HAFIZ)

**Hijab** *Lit. a veil.* It is usually used to describe the head-covering worn by women to maintain modesty. It was originally used to describe the curtain placed between the MOSQUE and the Prophet's living quarters to protect privacy. SUFIS also use the term to mean the veil that stands between Allah and His worshipper. (*See also* HIJAB AL-AZAMAH)

**Hijab al-Azamah** The veil that stands between Allah and His creation preventing human beings from seeing Him. It is believed by Muslims that Muhammad was taken right into the presence of God on his mystical Night Journey and therefore surpassed the experience of Moses who was denied the privilege of going past the veil. It is a common concept used in Sufism, which regards Muhammad as the ultimate mystic in his capacity as the final prophet of God. SUFI mystics themselves have modelled their lives on the Prophet in the hope of God being gracious enough to lift the veil that obscures His presence. (*See also* MI'RAJ; MUHAMMAD)

**Hijra** *Lit. emigration.* Muhammad left the troubled environment of MAKKAH and travelled to AL-MADINAH, arriving in September 622. Most of the loyal followers of the Prophet had made the journey ahead of him. The Islamic calendar begins from this event starting in June 622 and continuing through a lunar year based on 354 days. The idea of *Hijra* or flight from a non-Muslim environment in order to seek a more conducive place to practise the religion is recommended in the SHARI'A. (*See also* MUHAMMAD)

**Hira**  The name of the place outside MAKKAH where Muhammad went to pray and find solitude in a cave. The appearance of the angel JIBRIL and the first revelation of the QUR'AN are believed to have happened there. The cave remains an important site for Muslim pilgrims. (*See also* MUHAMMAD)

**Hirz**  *Lit. stronghold*. A word used in prayer to describe Allah as the shelter of the worshipper. It is also used in popular folk traditions to describe amulets containing verses of the QUR'AN that are used to ward off evil. (*See also* HIZB; TA'WIDH)

**Hizb**  A division of the QUR'AN usually associated with one-sixtieth of the content. It consists of petitions and prayers of the heart, arranged for recital and memorization. Alternatively known as *wird*, particular prayers are adopted by individual SUFI orders as part of their own liturgy of worship. However, they have also been used in folk tradition as formulas for magical protection or to control hostile forces in either nature or the supernatural. (*See also* HIRZ)

**Huda**  *Lit. guidance*. One of the titles of respect given to the QUR'AN that describes the function of the Revelation to provide correct guidance to human beings. Human reason or conscience are not considered to be reliable tools for knowing the correct path through life, and thus humanity requires the direct guidance and intervention of God.

**Hudud**  The part of SHARI'A law that deals with criminal law. Hudud offenses are those which are prescribed punishment in the QUR'AN such as theft, adultery and apostasy.

**Husain**  The grandson of Muhammad, son of ALI and FATIMA and brother of HASAN. He is regarded by SHI'A Muslims as the third IMAM and the fourth rightful leader of the Muslim community. The Shi'a believe that when MU'AWIYYA achieved the leadership of the Muslim community and established the UMAYYAD dynasty, he promised that on his death he would return the leadership of the community to Ali's children, Hasan and Husain. When Yazid succeeded to his father's throne, Husain led around 600 loyal followers to Damascus to claim the rightful leadership of the Muslim community. They were met by Yazid's army at Karbala in Iraq and slaughtered. The martyrdom of the grandson of Muhammad is commemorated on the annual occasion of MUHARRAM. Husain is regarded as the greatest of martyrs and has a redemptive role in Shi'a theology.

**Ibadah**  Muslim acts of worship or permissible actions performed with the intention to please Allah as they form part of His divine law. The ideal of *ibadah* would be to obey Allah's will in all realms of life. The word is derived from ABD (servant, slave) and denotes one whose attitude towards Allah is that of a servant or slave, maintained through worship.

**Iblis**  The JINN (sometimes described as an angel) who disobeyed Allah by refusing to bow to ADAM after his creation. He later becomes the tempter of all human beings until the final Day of Judgment. Iblis also exemplifies the dangers of the sin of pride.

**Ibrahim**  The Arabic form of Abraham. He is regarded as the exemplary Muslim and a prophet of God. Muhammad presented his early Muslim followers with a religion that was considered to be a return to the pure monotheism of Ibrahim and thus disassociated the fledgling community from the Jews or Christians. The QUR'AN describes Ibrahim as an UMMA (Godly community) by himself as Allah made a covenant with him as an individual rather than a religious community. He is believed to be father of three religions as a reward of his surrender and piety as exemplified in his willingness to sacrifice his son ISHMAEL. He is believed to be the founder of the KA'ABA in MAKKAH. (*See also* HAJAR; HAJJ)

**Id / Eid**  The two religious festivals or feasts to thank Allah. The two ids are celebrated at the end of RAMADAN and near the completion of the HAJJ. (*See also* ID AL-ADHA; ID AL-FITR)

**Id al-Adha / Eid al-Adha**   *Lit. the feast of sacrifice.* It is observed on the day when pilgrims to MAKKAH offer their sacrifice of goats in the valley of MINA near the completion of the HAJJ. The sacrifice remembers IBRAHIM's willingness to offer his son ISHMAEL to Allah. It is sometimes known as the Id al-Kabir or the greater Id.

**Id al-Fitr / Eid al-Fitr**   The festival that marks the completion of the RAMADAN month of fasting. It is celebrated on the first day of the Muslim month *Shawal*, the tenth month of the year, and begins with the first sighting of the new moon. It is also known as Id al-Saghir or the lesser Id although it is celebrated with more verve than the ID UL-ADHA. It is a joyous occasion after a long fast and gifts and cards are exchanged. It has sometimes been known as *Bairam*, after the practice of giving away sweetmeats to fellow Muslims and family members.

**Ihram**   The state or condition of purity required to perform the HAJJ when many actions normally permitted to Muslims are no longer allowed. The two pieces of plain cotton cloth which are worn by male pilgrims are also called *Ihram* to indicate the state of purity and equality that they share with each other. Women are expected to wear their normal modest clothing.

**Ihsan**   The ideal condition of a Muslim in prayer. It is explained in an HADITH attributed to Muhammad that a Muslim in prayer should be in a mental state that arises from the condition that the supplicant would be in if God was to appear in front of himself. If such a condition is not possible the Muslim should at least be aware that God sees the supplicant in front of Him. (*See also* TAQWA)

**Ijma**   The consensus of the community on a matter of law or practice. It is one of the four ways of arriving at a correct judgment concerning application of the Revelation to new matters. The decision is arrived at by a consensus of scholars. After the death of Muhammad, there was a vast body of material relating to the QUR'AN and the practice of the Prophet. When the UMAYYAD rulers assigned the task of legis- lation to acknowledged religious leaders, they realized that there was already in existence a large body of agreed practice. This was drawn upon in subsequent attempts at analogical reasoning to interpret correct practice in new situations. *Ijma* was perceived to be authoritative and even infallible to the degree that it actually defined right interpretation of the Qur'an and the SUNNA of the Prophet. This was based on a saying attributed to the Prophet: 'my community will never agree on an error'. (*See also* IJTIHAD; QIYAS; SHARI'A)

**Ijtihad**    An individual initiative by a qualified scholar to develop a response to a new situation by going direct to the QUR'AN and HADITH rather than to the existent body of law or FIQH. Although practised in the early years after the death of Muhammad, *ijtihad* was considered to be defunct or unreliable after the establishment of a body of law (*fiqh*) created largely on the authority of IJMA and QIYAS. The orthodox ULAMA declared the door of *ijtihad* to be closed. A limited form of *ijtihad* was allowed in that scholars could interpret laws already existing in their own school. Some rare scholars such as Ibn Taimiyya and Shah WALIALLAH maintained the right of *ijtihad*. In the contemporary Muslim world there is considerable debate over *ijtihad*, as a variety of modernist and revivalist thinkers have declared their right to perform the task. (*See also* SHARI'A)

**Ijtihad-nabawi**    The capacity of Muhammad to make individual decisions to resolve problems that were not discussed in the QUR'AN. It is believed by Muslims that the prophetic intelligence is endowed with wisdom and is of a greater capacity than ordinary human intelligence. (*See also* IJTIHAD; MUHAMMAD)

**Ikhwan al-Muslimun**    Founded in Egypt in 1928 by Hasan AL-BANNA (1906–1949), the Muslim Brotherhood, as it more commonly known, remains the prototype for all Islamist movements and the ideological wellspring for their activism. The movement works for the reform and revival of Islam following a conservative position based on a literalist interpretation of the foundational texts and the application of Islamic law in the state. This is combined with welfare programmes for the poor and needy. The movement continues to be influential in Egypt, operating in the political system as a powerful critic of the government and participating in elections.

**Ilm al-Nujum** *Lit. the science of the stars.* The art of astrology used either to produce horoscopes at the time of birth, to discover auspicious or inauspicious days for performimg activities, or to answer specific questions.

**Imam** In the SUNNI tradition of Islam, the title simply refers to one who leads the public prayers in the MOSQUE. Such a person is usually an ALIM who has completed full religious education in a MADRASA, but in the absence of a qualified IMAM, the eldest or most pious member of the community is called upon. Sometimes the title is conferred upon the founders of the four schools of law as an honorific. However, in the SHI'A tradition, the title of *imam* carries far more mystical and temporal weight as it is given to the Prophet's successors through the line of ALI and FATIMAH who are the spiritual leaders of the Shi'a community. They are believed to share in the Prophet's knowledge of the Unseen and to be the only correct interpreters of the inner meaning of the Qur'an. There are two main branches of SHI'A. The largest are the Ithna'ashariyya who acknowledge twelve *imams*, and the smaller group is the ISHMAELIS who acknowledge seven. The final *imam* in each group is believed to have been taken into a special place by Allah until before the final Day of Judgment. The final *imam* is represented in Shi'a by ayatollahs. (*See also* HASAN; HUSAIN; ITHNA'SHARIYA)

**Imam Khatib** The title used to differentiate an IMAM who leads the prayers from one who is a qualified ALIM. (*See also* IMAM RHATIB)

**Imam Rhatib** A qualified IMAM who is able to preach and instruct as well as lead the prayers. He will be an ALIM who has completed an eight-year course in a MADRASA. (*See also* IMAM KHATIB)

**Imamah** The office and function of the IMAM in the SHI'A tradition.

**Iman** *Lit. faith.* An essential component of being a MUMIN (believer). It refers also to the activity of belief which is necessary to follow the DIN or the path of Revelation. Muslim theologians identified three aspects of *iman*. The heart had to accept the articles of the faith; the lips uttered the SHAHADAH and gave vocal witness to the faith; the limbs performed the activities of the faith such as the five times obligatory prayer. (*See also* ISLAM; SHIRK)

**Injil**    The term used in the QUR'AN for the Gospels or the book of Revelation given to the Prophet (Jesus). However, it is believed that there was an original book given to Jesus as Revelation in the same manner as the QUR'AN was given to Muhammad. This book has been lost and the four Gospels of the Christian New Testament are, at best, attempts to recreate it. Since they have been reinterpreted by human inspiration rather than the direct words of God, they are not to be completely trusted. (*See also* ISA)

**Insan al-kamil**    *Lit. the perfect man.* Ibn ARABI developed the theosophy of the perfect man as embodied in the figure of Muhammad. The Prophet becomes the original creation which God uses as a mirror in order to admire Himself. This is achieved by the purity and sinlessness of the Prophet's heart. Muhammad is the bridge between the divine world and creation and the Divine Attributes and Names of Allah are reflected perfectly in his being and actions. In this role, the Prophet becomes the perfect model for Muslims, and especially the SUFI tradition, where devout adherents use Muhammad as the role model of the perfect mystic. (*See also* HAQIQA MUHAMMADIYYA; MUHAMMAD)

**Insh'Allah**    A very commonly used phrase that means 'by the will of God'. Muslims will interject it into most sentences that express an event in the future. For example, the sentence 'I will meet you tomorrow' would usually contain the conditional 'if Allah wills'.

**Iqama / Iqamah**    The call given in the MOSQUE by the IMAM that instructs the gathered congregation to stand up for SALAH or the five-times daily communal prayer.

**Iqra**    *Lit. recite or read.* The first commandment of the angel, Jibril, to Muhammad thus beginning the revelation of the QUR'AN. The important point here is that the *Qur'an* was revealed and recited by the Prophet rather than written by him. Tradition states that

Muhammad replied 'I do not read' or according to the translation, 'What shall I recite?'

**Isa**    The Arabic form of the name of Jesus who is highly regarded as a prophet of Allah who immediately preceded Muhammad, and who the QUR'AN describes as a Sign of Allah. Such an appellation is only given to Isa and the creation. It is considered that just as creation is able to remind the discerning of the existence and glory of Allah, so Isa, in his life, speech and presence, had a similar impact on those that met him. It is believed that Isa brought the Revelation to the Jewish people to remind them of their chosenness and to restore the heart to the law of Moses that was by then corrupted and dry. In the SUFI tradition, Isa has great status as a mystic and a practitioner of the TARIQA. Muslims believe in the virgin birth but do not accept that the Prophet of God would have received such an ignominious death as crucifixion and that a semblance was crucified through God's intervention. (*See also* RASUL)

**Isha (Salat-ul-Isha)**    The evening prayer, and the last of the five obligatory prayers that constitute SALAH, which may be performed from just over an hour after sunset up until midnight. (*See also* ASR; FAJR; MAGHRIB; ZUHR)

**Ishmael / Isma'il / Isamail**    The son of IBRAHIM (Abraham) and HAJAR and a prophet of Allah. He is believed to be the father of the Arab people and was miraculously shown the site of the ZAMZAM spring when stranded in the desert with his mother. He is therefore attributed with founding the city of MAKKAH. According to the QUR'AN he helped his father build the KA'ABA and he placed the black stone within it. Muslims believe that it was Ishmael, not Isaac, who was prepared for sacrifice by Ibrahim.

**Ishmaeli / Ishmaili / Ishma'ili**    A branch of SHI'A sometimes known as the Seveners because they believe that the seventh IMAM was the last and the greatest. The Ishma'ilis were the first major division of Shi'a and were concerned with a difference over leadership. Whereas the main group accepted MUSA, the son of the sixth *imam*, Ja'far (d. 765), a breakaway group disputed the new leadership and supported the elder son, Ishma'il, who was alleged to have drunk wine. It is Ishma'il who it is believed will one day return as the MAHDI. From the ninth to the eleventh century, the Ishma'ilis were strong throughout the Muslim world and established the FATAMID dynasty in Egypt. Nowadays, they are found predominantly in the Indian subcontinent and central Asia. The Ishma'ilis combine traditional Shi'a belief and practice with a theosophy based on esoteric interpretation of the QUR'AN which is highly influenced by emanationist theories deriving from Neo-platonism. The Ishma'ilis also differ radically from SUNNI and other Shi'a Muslims in that they do not accept the finality of Muhammad's prophethood. The Ishma'ilis are divided into two branches: the Musta'lis led by Muhammad Burhan al-Din in Bombay and the Nizaris led by the Aga Khan. (*See also* ITHNA'SHARIYA)

**Islah**   *Lit. reform.* A concept often drawn upon by revivalist movements in the twentieth century. It is the term used in the QUR'AN to describe the preaching of prophets who warn people of the need to return to God's ways. *Islah* is therefore defined as the effort to maintain the purity of the faith by increasing the righteousness of the people through various activities. (*See also* DA'WA; TAJDID)

**Islam**   The religious teaching, practice, faith and obedience to Allah based on the revelation of the QUR'AN and exemplified in the character and behaviour of the final Prophet Muhammad. Islam also means the state of submission or surrender to the Divine best achieved through practice of the above, although it is admitted in the historical tradition founded under Muhammad that there were always individuals that had attained to the state of Islam prior to the final Revelation. The epitome of this state of surrender would have been the prophet IBRAHIM. (*See also* AHL AL-KITAB; HANIF; MUHAMMAD)

**Isma**   The doctrine that Muhammad was protected from sin and error. Although not found in the earliest records of the faith or reflected in the HADITH, where the Prophet is often recorded praying for the forgiveness of his sins, later Muslim commentators began to develop the theology of sinlessness. It is generally accepted that absolute obedience to the Prophet can only be viable if Muhammad was free from any faults himself and thus able to provide an immaculate model. (*See also* INSAN AL-KAMIL; MUHAMMAD)

**Isnad**  The important chain of transmission that authenticates the HADITH by tracing them back to the Prophet through a line of authorities that heard the saying until it arrives back at a companion of the Prophet who would have heard it from Muhammad himself. The shorter the chain, the more authentic the *hadith*. In the eighth and ninth centuries, it became essential to authenticate the millions of sayings around the Muslim world. Various scholars collected and collated the *hadith* and attributed a chain to each one. Indisputable chains are considered the mark of authenticity. Each *hadith* is written with its chain.

**Istafta**  Legal queries concerned with problems that involve a decision being made on a point of religious law. These are made by members of the ULAMA on the basis of their knowledge of FIQH (jurisprudence). Some Muslims have claimed the right to independent reasoning but this remains rare. (*See also* IJTIHAD; MUJTAHID)

**Istighatha**  A form of TAWASSUL where the Muslim supplicant seeks assistance from the Prophet usually by calling for his intercession. (*See also* DU'A; SHAFA'A)

**Istihsan**  A category of independent reasoning (IJTIHAD) in which the MUJTAHID considered a certain course of action to be good and therefore permissible. (*See also* FIQH; ISTISHAB; ISTISLAH)

**Istikharat**  The term used for trusting in God to provide the right choice when faced with several options. (*See also* TARIQ AL-ISTIKHARAT)

**Istishab**  A category of independent reasoning (IJTIHAD) in which the MUJTAHID considered a certain course of action to be permissible by the use of analogy that linked it back to a provision in the QUR'AN or HADITH. (*See also* FIQH; ISTIHSAN; ISTISLAH)

**Istislah**  A category of independent reasoning (IJTIHAD) in which the MUJTAHID considered a certain course of action to be permissible by deeming that it was beneficial for the public good. (*See also* FIQH; ISTIHSAN; ISTISHAB)

**Istisqa**   A special prayer for rain in times of drought, especially used in Oriental Muslim nations such as those of the subcontinent. It is believed that Muhammad himself was the first to successfully pray for rain and the prayer is believed to be the same one that he used. (*See also* DU'A)

**Ithna'shariya**   The dominant form of Islam in Iran and the largest SHI'A group. Commonly known as the Twelver Shi'as because they acknowledge the succession of twelve IMAMS, beginning with ALI, as their spiritual leadership and as successors to Muhammad. (*See also* SHI'A)

**Itikaf**   A retreat maintained by the pious in the MOSQUE during the last ten days of RAMADAN. A small tent-like enclosure of white sheeting is wrapped around four poles. The individual Muslim performing the retreat will enter usually with a copy of the QUR'AN. They will remain there and only come out to join the congregation for the five ritual prayers. The most auspicious place to perform *itikaf* is the first mosque in AL-MADINAH established by Muhammad.

**Izzat (Urdu)**   The concept of honour or family pride. *Izzat* functions as an eclectic mixture of Islamic codes and local customs which the family members are expected to observe. Non-observance leads to disgrace for the individual and the family.

**Jabr** *Lit. predestination.* There was considerable debate between various groups after Muhammad's death concerning the issue of predestination and free will. The overriding mood in Islam is towards predestination as it is difficult to promote free will alongside Allah's omnipotence and omniscience. However, the early Muslims were aware of the tension between God's omnipotence and human moral responsibility. AL-ASHARI resolved the issue by declaring that the power to act belonged to God, but the specific choice of action belonged to human beings. (*See also* QADAR)

**Jahiliya / Jahiliyya / Jahiliyah / Jahiliyyah** *Lit. a time of ignorance.* The term used to describe pre-Islamic Arabia, especially the pagan culture of the tribes and the greed of the polytheistic merchants in MAKKAH. The concept of *jahiliya* as an infidel, godless society is sometimes extended to describe the non-Muslim world. It has been used by various modern revivalist movements to describe the West and provides a justification for JIHAD and DA'WA activities.

**Jalal** *Lit. majesty.* One of the two complimentary aspects or attributes of Allah and one of the ninety-nine divine names. The other aspect is JAMAL (beauty). It is the interplay of these two that keeps the universe in motion and maintains the flow of created life. Muhammad is believed by many traditional Muslims to have been endowed with both *jalal* and *jamal*. *Jalal* has been compared with Rudolf Otto's idea of the *tremendum* aspect of the Divine.

**Jamaat / Jami'at / Jamiyat**   *Lit. the party of God*. An Islamic group committed to DA'WA activities to promote the correct practice of Islam in the Muslim world. In this respect the term has a modern usage, but was originally used by Muhammad to describe the complete body of Muslims (*jama'at al-Muslimin*) or the totality of the body politic. (*See also* IKHWAN AL-MUSLIMUN; JAMAAT-I ISLAMI; TABLIGH-I JAMAAT)

**Jamaat-i Islami**   A movement founded in 1941 by Maulana MAWDUDI (1904–80) to provide youth with instruction in Islam. The Jamaat-i Islami was created to establish Mawdudi's vision of an Islamic state in Pakistan. Although it never achieved mass support, especially in rural areas, its organizational ability and attraction to the urban middle-classes provided it with enough influence to impact on various governments. The Jamaat-i Islami is essentially anti-clerical and recruits extensively from the universities of the subcontinent. They provide a similar model of organization and ideological belief to the IKHWAN AL-MUSLIMUN in Egypt founded by HASAN AL-BANNA.

**Jamaat-khana**   A gathering of disciples meeting with their SHAIKH to perform dhikr (remembrance of Allah) or listening to him preach. It would usually be inside the dwelling place of the *Shaikh* and his family. (*See also* TARIQA)

**Jamal**   *Lit. beauty*. One of the two complimentary aspects or attributes of Allah and one of the ninety-nine divine names. The other aspect is JALAL (majesty). It is the interplay of these two that keeps the universe in motion and maintains the flow of created life. Muhammad is believed by many traditional Muslims to have been endowed with both *jalal* and *jamal*. *Jamal* has been compared with Rudolf Otto's idea of the *fascinans* aspect of the divine.

**Jami'at / Jamiyat**   *See* JAMAAT.

**Jibril / Jibreel**   *Lit. Gabriel*. The angel who always appears to Allah's chosen prophets as the messenger of God. The revelation of the QU'RAN to Muhammad came through Jibril and Miriam (Mary) received a visitation when told that she was to give birth to ISA (Jesus).

**Jihad**   *Lit. striving*. The term refers to the duty imposed by the QUR'AN upon every Muslim to struggle against evil whilst walking the path of Allah. It is both the inner struggle against the manifestations of sin in oneself and the outer struggle to promote Islam and protect the faith against its enemies. In this latter context *jihad* has often been interpreted to be 'Holy war' either against polytheists, or Christians and Jews that threaten the security of Islam. A genuine *jihad* has to be carefully defined by criteria laid down in the SHARI'A and led by an IMAM or Muslim head of state. The main criterion is that it must be fought only to protect the faith and not be used for any lesser temporal motive. A famous saying of Muhammad states that after returning from fighting he told his companions that 'this was the lesser *jihad*, I will now show you the greater *jihad*'. It was explained that the latter *jihad* constituted the battle against carnal desire and the purification of the inner being. The emphasis on the inner *jihad* has been mostly followed by the SUFIS. Some twentieth-century revivalist movements have declared *jihad* the sixth pillar of Islam. They are usually emphasizing the duty of Muslims to struggle to promote their faith amongst lapsed members of the community and the apparent threat to Islamic values from globalization of Western values. (*See also* JAHILIYA; SHAHID)

**Jinn**   A supernatural life form that Allah created from fire as opposed to humankind who were created from earth. Tradition states that Muhammad was sent to preach to them and some became Muslims. It is even stated that Muhammad first believed that he was under attack by *jinn* when he received the first revelations of the QUR'AN. There are many IMAMS who are taught how to exorcise bad *jinns* during their training at the DAR AL-ULUM or religious schools. In village traditions, *jinn* are often blamed for mental and physical illnesses and misfortune.

**Jizya**   Islamic law indicates that a reasonable tax should be levied on DHIMMI or the 'People of the Book' within a Muslim nation in order to pay for defence and the administration of the state. Non-Muslims are required to pay ZAKAH and should be given complete religious, political and administrative freedom. (*See also* AHL-AL-KITAB)

**Juba**    A cloak of wool traditionally given by a PIR or SHAIKH in the SUFI tradition to his successor or KHALIFA. (*See also* SILSILA)

**Julus (Urdu)**    A procession of Muslims traditionally held on the day celebrating Muhammad's birthday. This is an event usually associated with the SUFI tradition and is often led by SHAIKHS accompanied by their MURIDS (followers). It has been associated with sacralizing space and is often carried out in cities in Britain where there are strong subcontinent communities of Muslims. (*See also* BARELWI; MAULID)

**Juma / Jumu'ah (Salat-ul-Jumu'ah) / Juma Namaz (Urdu)**    The weekly communal prayer and attendance at the KHUTBA (sermon) held on Friday shortly after midday and completed by 2pm, which is traditionally expected to be the minimum attendance at the MOSQUE for those who pray at work or in the home.

**Junayd**    (d. 910) IMAM Junayd al-Baghdadi was born in Persia but went on to become the chief judge of Baghdad after studying law in the city. He was a famous SUFI who taught that inner striving should be undertaken to return to one's source that was Allah. Many Sufi orders trace their lineage through him and he is reported to have said: 'If I had known any science greater than Sufism, I would have gone to it even on my hands and knees.' Junayd's most famous disciple was Mansur al-HALLAJ who was executed for blasphemy. It was Junayd who signed his death warrant as the Chief Judge of Baghdad.

# K

**Ka'aba / Ka'bah**  A cube-shaped structure which is the sacred shrine in MAKKAH. This is the point to which all Muslims face in prayer and which is circumambulated by pilgrims at the time of the HAJJ. It is believed to be the first house built for the worship of the one God and constructed by IBRAHIM and ISHMAEL. Muslims believe that the Makkan ruling tribes had turned the original high alter to the worship of one God into a place for the worship of idols that had been installed in the *Ka'aba*. Muhammad, as a part of his prophetic role, restored the ancient place of worship to the one God and threw out the idols. The *Ka'aba* is twelve metres long, eleven metres wide and fifteen metres high. The cube itself is covered by a black cloth into which the SHAHADAH is interwoven. This cloth is renewed every year. The black stone which is believed to be a meteorite is set in the east corner of the *ka'aba*. (*See also* SALAH)

**Kafir**  *See* KUFR.

**Kalam**  Classical Muslim theology that developed in the first centuries after Muhammad as various factions debated issues raised by the message of the QUR'AN and the prevailing political situation. The major concerns of *kalam* were predestination, free will and the nature of good and evil, the unity of God and His Attributes and the eternality of the QUR'AN. The major schools were the MURJI'ITES, MU'TAZILITES and the ASHARITES.

**Kalima / Kalimah**  *See* SHAHADAH.

**Karama / Karamat**   The supernatural power from Allah that is given to a prophet or a WALI (SUFI saint) that enables him to perform miracles. (*See also* BARAKA)

**Karbala**   An important shrine of the SHI'A situated in Iraq. It was the site of the martyrdom of HUSAIN, the grandson of the Prophet and the third IMAM. He had marched with a small number of followers to overthrow the UMAYYAD dynasty after the death of MU'AWIYYA. This event is marked every year in the festival of MOHARRAM.

**Kashf**   Discovery or knowledge that comes through illumination rather than reason and the basis of the mystical path or Sufism. In this form of knowing, the meaning of faith and truth is given in experiential immediacy direct to the soul without going first to the intellect. AL-GHAZALI defended *kashf* as the most certain form of knowledge. (*See also* SUFI)

**Khadijah**   The first wife of the Prophet and mother of his daughter FATIMAH. Khadijah was a widow who had inherited her deceased husband's business as a merchant. Muhammad, who was known for trustworthiness, managed caravans for her. She was the first to accept the Revelation of the QUR'AN and the prophethood of Muhammad and supported Muhammad in the first years in MAKKAH when the fledgling community faced many difficulties. Tradition states that the Prophet was initially terrified by the Revelation of the *Qur'an* and the presence of the Angel JIBRIL. He ran from his place of retreat and hid and trembled in Khadijah's skirts. She died before the HIJRA to AL-MADINAH. (*See also* AISHA)

**Khalifa / Khalifah / Caliph**   The successors to the Prophet. They do not inherit the mantle of Prophethood but lead the Muslim community. The first Caliph was ABU BAKR and he and the three Caliphs that followed are known as the four righteous ones. After the death of ALI, the UMAYYAD Caliphate came into existence and transferred the capital of the empire to Damascus. It was superseded by the ABBASID Caliphate in 750 whose Caliphs ruled from Baghdad until 1258. After the invasion of the Mongols and the collapse of the Muslim empires into sultanates, there was no effective Caliphate although the succession was maintained and disputed in various parts of the Muslim world. In 1517, the OTTOMANS removed the Caliphate to Istanbul, from where it was finally abolished by Mustapha Kemal (Ataturk) in 1924. Today, there are small movements who wish a return to a Caliphate and a decline in the prominence of nation over UMMA. The term can also be used to signify the position of humankind as the vice-regent of Allah in the world. It is the God-given role of human beings to maintain Allah's rule over creation. (*See also* AL-KHALIFA-UR-RASHIDUN, UMAR, UTHMAN)

**Khan, Sayyid Ahmad**  (1817–96) A Muslim modernist, who, after the 1857 mutiny or war of independence against the British in India, opposed the futility of militant opposition. Sayyid Ahmad Khan chose instead to focus on encouraging Indian Muslims to close ranks by overcoming ethnic and regional differences and to cooperate with the British rulers. Concerned to modernize Muslim education in line with Western education, he founded the famous Aligarh University. In a break with traditional Islam, he advocated that the QUR'AN be interpreted to remove all apparent contradictions with scientific truths. He believed that any passages that conflicted with demonstrative truth should be regarded as metaphorical. While his ideas were not received well by traditionalists, he is still revered as one of the first exponents of Muslim nationalism. His loyalty to the British won him a knighthood, which has not endeared him to contemporary Muslim revivalist movements (*See also* MUHAMMAD ABDUH; JAMAL AL-DIN AFGHANI; MAULANI MAWDUDI)

**Khanqah**  *See* DAR.

**Kharijite**  A number of Muslim sectarian movements that developed during the time of the third and fourth Caliphs but flourished during the regime of MU'AWIYYA, the first UMAYYAD Caliph. Opposed to the wealth and irreligious lifestyles of the Umayyad rulers they withdrew from the wider Muslim community and lived together practising a lifestyle which they believed was based on that of Muhammad and his companions. The main difference with other Muslims concerned the authority of leadship. Whereas the SUNNI community had placed the leadership in a succession of Caliphs who had become, in effect, monarchs, and the SHI'A community believed that leadership belonged to a mystical understanding of the Prophet's bloodline, the Kharijite movements believed that the community should appoint the leader on the basis of piety. He could also be removed by the community if felt to be inadequate. Their major contribution was their belief that Muslims who are disobedient to the Revelation were apostates and guilty of treason against the community. They argued that all true believers were obliged to wage JIHAD against nominal or self-styled Muslims. (*See also* AZRAQITES)

**Khatam al-anbiya** *Lit. the seal of the prophets.* The important and central doctrine that Muhammad is the last of the messengers of God who has received the final complete revelation for all human beings contained in the QUR'AN. This is a qualitative as well as quantitative distinction because the final Prophet manifests the complete and perfected character of all the prophets. (*See also* MUHAMMAD; NABI; RASUL)

**Khatib** A religious specialist who is appointed to a large MOSQUE as the deliverer of the Friday sermon. Such preachers have an important role in that they are able to bring the text of the QUR'AN and the sayings of the HADITH to everyday life. Most mosques would not be able to support an independent *khatib* and his function will be performed by the IMAM. (*See also* KHUTBA)

**Khawass** The magical properties contained within an object, especially plants that could be called upon by healers.

**Khilafa** The institution of the Caliphate. (*See also* KHALIFA)

**Khirqa-i Sharif** The supposed cloak of Muhammad, found as a holy relic in several MOSQUES around the Muslim world including Kandahar in Afghanistan, Kuldabad in India, and, most famously, in the Topkapi Museum in Istanbul. (*See also* MUHAMMAD)

**Khojah** A trading community of Hindu converts found mainly in the state of Sind in Pakistan or Gujarat in India. They are mainly ISHMAELIS but some of them have moved into Twelver SHI'A as practised in Iran. Migration from Gujarat to East Africa and other parts of the world has resulted small Khojah communities in Britain, Canada and the USA.

**Khomeini, Ayotollah** (d. 1989) The SHI'A cleric who was the architect of the Islamic revolution in Iran. He had been exiled to France in the 1960s by the Shah. He returned in triumph in 1979 and became the leader of the new Iranian Islamic republic. He condemned Western imperialism and the globalization of Western culture which he saw as threatening to Islamic identity. He proposed an Islamic state opposed to all Western forms of governance within Muslim nations, including monarchy. He affirmed the unity of Islam and politics and proposed that the Shi'a Muslim clerics should participate in government. Islamic polity must be based on the rule of the SHARI'A and therefore the best ruler would be one most qualified in interpreting Islamic jurisprudence. After an initial struggle Khomeini and his followers prevailed. The Shah was overthrown and Iran was declared an Islamic state. (*See also* AYATOLLAH)

**Khums** A donation to charity or to a Muslim state treasury which is in addition to ZAKAH. SUNNI Muslims consider that it is only payable on booty gathered in warfare or a percentage of income gained from natural resources; whereas SHI'A Muslims regard it as an extra payment of one-fifth of one's surplus annual income. (*See also* SADAQAH)

**Khutba / Khutbah** The sermon delivered at the JUMA prayers on Friday or at the ID celebrations. The sermon generally follows a set pattern and is exhortary in its tone. It rarely analyses or even provides exegesis. The general assumption is that believers know what is required but forget to do it. Many MOSQUE preachers follow a set theme based on the time of the year and traditionally may comment on political and state affairs. This will vary from Muslim state to state in contemporary society depending on the relationship between religion and state. There are also published collections of sermons. (*See also* IMAM; KHATIB)

**Kihana**   The art of divination used to predict events but not usually to alter them, the latter remaining the province of SIHR.

**Kitab**   *Lit. a book*. Although the term is used to describe any book, Islam is a religion of the Book and has a deep respect for the written word. Revelation from God comes in its highest form as a divine Book passed to a messenger who embodies its teachings. There are four such books respected and revered in Islam – TAWRAH, INJIL, ZABUR and QUR'AN. The first three (Torah, Psalms and Gospels) are believed to have been corrupted by human error entering the original revelation and only the *Qur'an* is perfect and complete. (*See also* AHL-I KITAB)

**Kufr**   Someone who rejects revelation and has disbelief in God and his signs. It is the ultimate sin along with SHIRK (worshipping something other than God). There has been considerable debate over who is to be declared *kufr*. Most generally, it is used as a term to describe non-Muslims but this is problematic as the QUR'AN gives special status to Christians and Jews as People of the Book. Various factions within Islam have labelled each other as *kufr* based on their acceptance of certain beliefs that divide the various movements in Islam. (*See also* AHL-I KITAB; KHARIJITES)

**Kun**   *Lit. be!* The mystic word that reflects how God gives birth to creation. The Divine imperative calls everything into existence and maintains it until the command is withdrawn. Thus the command to existence is not in the past tense as an event that took place in history but is the agency of creation in this present moment.

**La ilaha illa Allah**   *Lit. there is no god but God.* The first part of the SHAHADAH or the witnessing that defines someone as a Muslim. It is also the most common form of DHIKR (remembrance of Allah) repeated rhythmically by the followers of SUFI TARIQAS as a means of purification and emotional expression of their love. Although a simple statement of monotheism there are different emphases made by diverse movements in the Muslim world that express their own tradition of belief and practice. Maulana MAWDUDI, for example, provided an exegesis of sovereignty which becomes a political statement opposing ideologies such as nationalism or secular democracy as ideologies that do not acknowledge the mood of Islam to offer allegiance only to God's law. Sufi traditions, on the other hand, are more likely to perceive the statement in mystical terms as a tool for transformation. Here the mood of interpretation is more inclined towards monism – nothing exists except God.

**Labbaika**   *Lit. here I am before you.* The greeting, known as the *Talbiya*, uttered by Muslims on their arrival in MAKKAH for the HAJJ, after they have donned their white garment and entered the sanctified state of the pilgrim. It is repeated throughout the pilgrimage.

**Laylat-ul-Qadr**   *Lit. the night of power.* The night that the first revelation of the QUR'AN was given to Muhammad in the cave above MAKKAH where he used to go regularly for retreat. Muslims believe it to be one of the last ten days of RAMADAN and it is considered one of the most sacred days of the fast. This is the day when, in a sense, God came down to earth and intervened in human history by revealing his final prophet and rewarding him with the last revelation. Traditionally, Muslims believe that the day in which this event is celebrated is distinguished by a loosening of the boundaries between the world and the Divine. The angels are still believed to descend to the holy places of Islam and many believe that it is easier to experience the transcendent on this day than any other. (*See also* JIBRIL; MUHAMMAD)

# M

**Madhab**  The term given to the variety of movements that form various schools of Islamic thought. It can also be applied to the four different schools of law. The term is not as strong as 'sectarian' since all the various schools of thought are considered to be members of the Muslim community, but rivalries between them can be strong. (*See also* BARELWI; DEOBAND; HANBALI; HANAFI; JAMAAT; MALIKI; SHAFI'I; SUFI)

**Madinah**  *See* AL-MADINAH.

**Madrasa / Madrasah / Madrassa / Madrassah**  A school for religious study usually attached to a MOSQUE and teaching a curriculum that extends from study of the QUR'AN and HADITH through to Islamic jurisprudence, recitation, FIQH (schools of law) and sometimes logic. Muslim minorities in non-Muslim countries would probably include language study in Arabic or the vernacular language of the country of origin. The full graduates of the eight-year course of study are known as ULAMA and are qualified to become IMAMS of mosques and make judgments on issues of Islamic law. The *madrasa* system was established thoughout the Muslim world by the twelfth century and in many ways contributed to the unity of the Muslim world-view and the maintenance of SHARI'A law after the collapse of the ABBASID empire and the disintegration of the Caliphate after the invasion of the Monguls. (*See also* DAR AL-ULUM; DARS I-NIZAMI)

**Maghrib (Salat ul-Maghrib)**  The fourth of the obligatory five-times daily prayers which is held at sunset. They can be recited from after sunset until darkness falls. (*See also* ASR; FAJR; ISHA; SALAT; ZUHR)

**Mahabba**   The reciprocal love that exists between Allah and His creation. The ideal of the lover and the Beloved is strong in Sufism where the lover yearns to be drawn into the flame of the Divine and lose all individual identity. It is believed that a stage is reached where the role is reversed and the Beloved yearns to be His lover. In this stage God reaches out in grace towards the ardent devotee. (*See also* FANA; MAHBUB; SUFI)

**Mahbub, al-**   The name of Allah that refers to His divine attribute of the 'Beloved', the goal of the heart's aspiration being to lose itself in Divine love. (*See also* FANA; MAHABBA)

**Mahdi al-Muntaz**   The messianic figure who is awaited and will appear towards the end of time to lead the Muslim UMMA and restore Islam throughout the world as the first and final religion of God. He will be accompanied by ISA (Jesus). Muslims believe that he is the fulfilment of the prophesy of a messiah contained within Jewish and Christian traditions. In the SHI'A tradition, the Mahdi is believed to be the return of the last IMAM who was taken into occultation, or removal to a Divine place of safety, in order to protect him from persecution and assassination.

**Majlis**   A gathering or assembly of Muslims usually coming together for the purposes of religion. The term is also used in the SUFI tradition to describe a collection of a saint's sayings or aphorisms. When Muslims are gathered together for the remembrance of Allah through the recital of His names, it is known as *majlis adh-dhikr* (a gathering for the recollection of God). In contemporary Islam, *majlis* often take the shape of a conference with several invited inspirational or scholarly speakers. (*See also* DHIKR; WALI)

**Majnun**   A term used to describe someone who is possessed. The positive use of the term refers to someone who is overwhelmed by God or in a condition of ecstasy. For example, a magician heard that Muhammad was described a *majnun*, but when he approached him with offers to exorcise his demons, Muhammad replied that he trusted completely in God.

**Makkah / Mecca**  The foremost of the holy cities for all Muslims. It is the city where the KA'ABA is situated and the direction in which all Muslims face when performing the obligatory SALAH (five-times-a-day ritual prayer). All Muslims are expected to attend the HAJJ or pilgrimage to the city at least once in their lives if it is financially or physically possible. The city of Makkah is associated with many key religious events in the history of the revelations believed to have been given to humanity. It is believed that ADAM and Eve were given God's mercy and forgiveness in the hills that surround the city. Makkah itself was founded by the miraculous appearance of the ZAMZAM spring that saved HAGAR and ISHMAEL. The *Ka'aba* itself is believed to have been established as a place of worship by IBRAHIM when visiting his other family. More importantly, Muhammad was born in the city and began to receive the first revelations of the QUR'AN's verses there. Although opposed by the city's merchants he finally entered the city in triumph in 630 and performed the pilgrimage after destroying the idols at the *Ka'aba* shrine. Makkah provides a geographical focal point of worship which helps supply a sense of unity for Muslims everywhere and reinforces the ideal of the UMMA (universal community of believers). (*See also* MUHAMMAD)

**Maktab / Maktub**  A school for children to study the QUR'AN usually attached to the MOSQUE. In Britain and other Muslim minority communities, the school is for two hours in the early evening after the daytime schooling has finished. Children are usually instructed by the IMAM in recitation and memorization of the *Qur'an*; correct performance of the rituals of the religion; and basic knowledge of Islamic beliefs, practices and morality. (*See also* MADRASA; DAR AL-ULUM)

**Malfuzat**  A collection of a saint's writings taken down by disciples from their experiences of being together with him informally at meals or other occasions. (*See also* MANAQIB; SUFI; WALI)

**Maliki**  One of the four orthodox schools of law in SUNNI Islam founded by Malik ibn Anas (d. 795) in AL-MADINAH. At present this school of Muslim law is dominant in North and West Africa and Upper Egypt. Malik ibn Anas built the school of law on the principle of relying upon living traditions practiced in al-Madinah that were authenticated and supported by HADITH. (*See also* HANBALI; HANAFI; SHAFI'I)

**Manaqib**    Hagiographical accounts of a saint's life or works that describe their virtues and merits. These can be combined with MALFUZAT (informal collections of their conversations) to produce larger biographical texts. (*See also* WALI)

**Manqulat**    Traditional sciences of studying QUR'AN and HADITH which formed part of the DARS I NIZAMI curriculum taught in the mediaeval *madrasas* and still maintained in many MADRASAS to this day, particularly in the Indian subcontinent. (*See also* DAR AL-ULUM; MA'QULAT)

**Maqam / Maqamat**    The various stages of spiritual development leading to FANA through which a SUFI adherent can progress under the guidance of a master. The term also refers to a place where a saint has manifested his presence and can be communicated with by those seeking his guidance or spiritual blessings. (*See also* AHWAL; HAQIQA; MAZAR; WALI)

**Ma'qulat**    The rational sciences of logic and philosophy which formed the other half of the DARS I NIZAMI curriculum in addition to MANQULAT, the study of QUR'AN and HADITH. The curriculum was taught in the mediaeval MADRASAS and is still maintained to this day, particularly in the Indian subcontinent. (*See also* DAR AL-ULUM)

**Ma'rifa**    Esoteric knowledge that is arrived at by direct perception or apprehension of God experienced by the SUFI adherent as a result of practising the spiritual techniques of Sufism under the guidance of a qualified master. (*See also* DHIKR; FANA; HAQIQAT; SHAIKH; WALI)

**Marwah**    *See* SAFA.

**Maryam**    Mary, the virgin mother of ISA (Jesus) who was visited by the angel JIBRIL to announce the birth of her son. The QUR'AN states that she was given to the Temple as a virgin but was accused of giving birth to an illegitimate child. Her spotless reputation was preserved by the miraculous defence of his mother by the newly born Isa. Maryam is proclaimed by the *Qur'an* to be the foremost of women and therefore occupies the highest status given to any woman in the tradition, even above that of Muhammad's wives.

**Masjid**   *Lit. a place of prostration.* This is an alternative title for a MOSQUE or Muslim place of worship.

**Mathnawi**   The famous inspired poetical work of Jalud'din RUMI (d. 1273) that consists of spiritual anecdotes, ecstatic utterances and parables that explore the inner relationship of the SUFI with Allah. It is known in Iran as the 'QUR'AN in Persian' and is regarded as an exposition of the esoteric meaning of the *Qur'an*.

**Maulana / Mawlana / Maulvi**   A title usually reserved for Muslim religious scholars who have completed the syllabus of a MADRASA and gone on to become members of the ULAMA and are knowledgeable concerning the QUR'AN, HADITH and Islamic jurisprudence. (*See also* FIQH)

**Maulid / Milad an(e) Nabi**   The birthday of Muhammad celebrated on the twelfth night of Rabi'al-awwal, the third lunar month of the Muslim calendar. Even in the early reports, miraculous events were associated with the Prophet's birthday and the tradition of celebrating it goes back at least as far the FATIMID dynasty in Egypt (969–1171). It is generally observed with prayer meetings, sermons and songs in praise of the Prophet, alms giving, distribution of sweets and sometimes illumination and processions. The celebration has always been of special significance to SUFIS but some orthodox theologians have declared the celebrations to be BID'A (innovation). It was especially criticized by the orthodox reformer, Ibn Taimiyya (d. 1328) and continues to be dismissed by the WAHABIS and SALAFIS. In spite of the criticism, the day of celebration is observed throughout the Muslim world with the notable exception of Saudi Arabia.

**Maulvi**   *See* MAULANA.

**Mawali**   *Lit. client or freedman.* The term applied to non-Arab Muslims when Islam first spread beyond the Arabian peninsula into Persia. Initially, the Mawali were taxed by their Arab conquerors and therefore felt resentment insofar as their treatment went against the supposed equality of the Muslim community. The resentment was expressed against the UMAYYAD dynasty and was one of the factors in the empire's downfall and its replacement by the ABBASID dynasty.

**Mawdudi, Maulana**   (1904–80) A Muslim journalist and the foremost thinker and activist of the twentieth-century Islamic revival. He was born in Hyderabad, India, but moved to Lahore when the partition of India and Pakistan took place. Bitterly opposed to nationalism, democracy, socialism and secularism as Western imports into the Muslim world, he argued that Muslim nations should develop a form of governance based upon the Islamic Revelation and the strict observance of Islamic law (SHARI'A). His main argument rested upon the sovereignty of Allah as central to Islam. Therefore any attempt to promote systems of government based upon the sovereignty of the people was tantamount to SHIRK, the sin of idolatry. As an activist, Mawdudi believed that the best minds of the Muslim world should be trained to form a JIHAD movement to bring about Islamic revolution. In 1941, he formed the organization JAMAAT-I ISLAMI to actualize his vision and work towards the Islamicization of the law, and on the founding of the state of Pakistan. (*See also* HASAN AL-BANNA)

**Mawlana**   *See* MAULANA.

**Mawlawi / Mevlevi**   The SUFI order founded in Turkey and established in Konya by Jalala'd-din RUMI after his meeting with the wandering dhervish, Shams al-Tabriz in 1244. The Mawlawi TARIQA expanded throughout the Seljuk and OTTOMAN empires and eventually became an influential part of the establishment as its SHAIKHS came to advisory positions in the empire. However, its wider fame came through its spiritual reputation and mystical practices, especially the use of distinctive music and dance to express and induce ecstasy. The order became famous throughout Europe as the 'whirling dervishes'.

**Mazar**  A tomb of a holy man or woman that has become a shrine. They may range from small domed tombs local to a village containing the body of a righteous or pious Muslim to grand edifices in large complexes also containing a MOSQUE, religious schools, hostels and functioning as centres of worship and SUFI teaching. The tombs exist throughout the Muslim world but the most famous is the tomb of Muhammad in AL-MADINAH. Other tombs are believed to be the burial place of earlier prophets or famous Sufi saints. Millions will gather at the more famous tombs especially on the occasion of the saint's birthday (URS). Most traditional Muslims believe that the tomb of a saint or prophet can be used as place for prayers of intercession. (*See also* DARGAH; KHANQAH; ZAWIYA)

**Mecca**   *See* MAKKAH.

**Medina**   *See* AL-MADINAH.

**Mevlevi**   *See* MAWLAWI.

**Mihrab**   The niche or alcove in the wall of the MOSQUE that faces towards MAKKAH. Traditionally the IMAM stands in front of the *Mihrab* to lead the communal prayers. (*See also* QIBLA)

**Milad an(e) Nabi**   *See* MAULID.

**Mina**   A plain near MAKKAH which is included in the city's area for the performance of some of the obligatory rituals of the HAJJ. On the tenth day of the pilgrimage each pilgrim casts seven stones upon a large heap to symbolize IBRAHIM's stoning of the devil as he tried to tempt the prophet from sacrificing his son. The stoning ends the official pilgrimage and opens the celebration of the Great Festival or ID AL-ADHA.

**Minaret**   The tower on the MOSQUE from which the MU'ADHIN traditionally makes the prayer-call five times a day, although nowadays it is more likely to be transmitted by a recording via a loudspeaker. The design of the minaret varies from place to place in the Muslim world but the most typical is a long, narrow circular tower with a pointed top and an opening for the MU'ADHIN near the summit. (*See also* ADHAN)

**Minbar**   The platform or chair from which the IMAM delivers the Friday sermon or KHUTBA at JUMA prayers.

**Miqat**   *Lit. place appointed*. The place where pilgrims enter into the state of IHRAM or ritual purity in preparation for the HAJJ. This must be completed somewhere after departure and before entering the precincts of MAKKAH. Many pilgrims enter the state of *ihram* at the edge of the city and herald their arrival with the cry of 'LABBAIKA'.

**Mi'raj**   *Lit. ladder*. The term refers to the ascent of Muhammad through the heavens in which he is transported from MAKKAH to Jerusalem and then uplifted to the very throne of God. The Night Journey, as it is known, is referred to in the QUR'AN in SURA 17: *Praise be He who travelled by night with his servant from the sacred mosque to the farthest sanctuary*. The earliest biography of the Prophet describes how Muhammad, accompanied by the angel JIBRIL, was taken by a heavenly mount to Jerusalem where he leads all the former prophets in prayer. After this he is taken on a mystical journey through all the levels of heaven and finally enters Paradise. For SUFIS, it is this experience that sets the Prophet out as a supreme mystic and marks him above Moses who was not able to enter God's presence. The MI'RAJ is celebrated annually on the 27th day of Rajab, the seventh lunar month, and, like the birthday celebration, it is regarded as a day of illumination in which MOSQUES are decorated with lamps. (*See also* MAULID; BURAQ)

**Mogul / Moghul / Moghal**   One of the three great Muslim empires which lasted from the sixteenth to the nineteenth century. The Mogul dynasty was established in India in 1526 when Babar, the ruler of Afghanistan, captured Delhi. By the reign of Akbar (1556–1605) the empire expanded to cover most of India. Although in decline, the last effective emperor was Aurangzeb who found himself increasingly under attack from the Marathas and the Sikhs. The empire of the Moguls lasted until 1857 when the British removed the last emperor. (*See also* OTTOMAN; SAFAVID)

**Moharram / Muharram**   The first month of the lunar year in which is held the festival that marks the tragedy at KARBALA when HUSAIN, the grandson of Muhammad, was martyred in 680. This is the major occasion for SHI'A Muslims who mark it by performing passion plays which dramatically represent Husain's suffering; renderings of grief-stricken poems; and processions in which adult males flagellate their backs to empathize with the suffering of the ultimate martyr. The occasion is also marked by most Muslims in the Indian subcontinent who, as a result of SUFI influence, hold the family of Muhammad in great regard.

**Mosque**   The building erected or used for public prayer. The name is derived from MASJID. The first mosque was the place built for community prayer and gatherings in AL-MADINAH. It was also Muhammad's home. Essentially a mosque is built on an axis which points to the KA'ABA. The basic features are a hall for prayer, a pulpit for the Friday sermon, a niche to point the direction of MAKKAH, and a source of water for ritual washing before prayer. However, the minimum requirement is a rectangle drawn in the sand with a niche to point the direction to Makkah. The large mosques built by various Muslim rulers were far more elaborate and contained MINARETS, calligraphy and splendid domes. (*See also* ADHAN; MIHRAB; MINBAR; MU'ADHIN; QIBLA; SALAT; WUDU)

**Mu'adhin / Muezzin**   The Muslim elected to call the faithful to prayer by reciting the ADHAN. Muhammad decided that the human voice should be the distinctive mark of the Muslim call to prayer as opposed to the bells of Christianity and the ram's horn of Judaism. He appointed BILAL, the black Ethiopian freed slave, as the first *mu'adhin*. Usually the call is made from the MINARET of the mosque but in places where Muslims are a minority, such as Western Europe, it may be completed in the mosque just prior to the prayer.

**Mu'amala**   Outward religious duties distinct from the obligatory rites of the religion as laid down in the SHARI'A. It is also used by some SUFIS to describe the outer or exoteric manifestations of Islam. (*See also* IBADAH; TARIQA)

**Mu'awiyah**   The founder of the UMAYYAD Caliphate in 661 when he succeeded after the death of ALI. Mu'awiyah moved the centre of the Muslim world away from AL-MADINAH to his own power base in Damascus and designated his son as his successor to the Caliphate, thereby founding a hereditary dynasty. There were many devout Muslims among the companions of Muhammad who regarded Mu'awiyah as an usurper and a corrupter of Islamic values. Others saw his military and expansionist successes as further proof of Allah's favour.

**Mu'azzimun**   Specialist exorcists who seek God's assistance to heal various conditions such as epilepsy or insanity believed to be caused through possession by evil spirits or JINN. (*See also* SAHIR)

**Muezzin**   *See* MU'ADHIN.

**Mufti**   A Muslim legal scholar or lawyer, either private or public, who is able to apply interpretation of the SHARI'A to individual cases. In time large numbers of individual case-laws became collections that could be used by Muslim judges in deciding cases that came before the courts. (*See also* QADI)

**Muhajir**   Indian Muslims who migrated to Pakistan in 1947 at the time of the partition of the subcontinent. They see themselves as a deprived minority in modern Pakistan and have organized themselves politically to obtain equal rights.

**Muhammad**   *Lit. praised.* The name of the final Prophet who was born in MAKKAH around 570. Somewhere around the age of forty he began to receive a series of revelations in which he was commanded to recite the QUR'AN, the final book of God containing the complete instruction which leads to submission and obedience to God's will. In 622, he departed for AL-MADINAH where he organized his followers into the first Muslim community that went on to spread the message of Islam very successfully throughout the Arabian peninsula and, after Muhammad's death, throughout the world. All Muslims acknowledge Muhammad as the final Prophet of God and the exemplar of Muslim belief and practice. The SUNNA or behaviour of the Prophet is second only to the *Qur'an* as a Divine source of guidance. However, millions of Muslims look to Muhammad as a perfect intercessor for their prayers to Allah and believe that he will also intercede for his community at the Day of Judgment. It is also traditionally believed that Muhammad is sinless and pre-existed creation as the Light of Allah. In the SUFI tradition, he is the ultimate mystic or saint as well as the final Prophet. The Prophet's tomb in al-Madinah is regarded as the second most holy shrine in Islam and is visited by millions of Muslims every year. (*See also* ISTIGHATHA; NA'T; NOOR; RASUL)

**Muharjihun**   *Lit. the emigrants.* The original Muslims, around one hundred and forty, who elected to leave MAKKAH and depart with the Prophet to AL-MADINAH and therefore shared in the HIJRA.

**Muharram**   *See* MOHARRAM.

**Mujaddid**   A devout Muslim popularly believed to renew the faith every hundred years by restoring it to its original purity. It is also believed that a special *mujaddid* appears every thousand years.

**Mujahada**   One of the mainstays of the mystical or SUFI path, it refers to the ideal of striving after perfection or complete purification of the heart. It is also used to describe mortification or penance undertaken to grapple with the unregenerate NAFS. In Sufism, *mujahada* is associated with JIHAD.

**Mujahiddin**   Muslims engaged in JIHAD or armed struggle to defend Islam. The term is often used by militant Islamic groups struggling to restore Islamic law and behaviour to various Muslim nations, or those involved in freedom struggles such as in Afghanistan or Kashmir.

**Mujawar / Mujawir**   The attendants at a shrine of a SUFI or Muslim holy man / woman. They are usually descendents of the person in the tomb and achieve their position on a hereditary basis. They will look after the shrine and guide the pilgrims to attend in worship and petition. Often the families will control the stalls from which offerings can be purchased and the guesthouses where pilgrims are accommodated. (*See also* DARGAH; MAZAR; SAJJADA NASHIN)

**Mu'jiza**    The miracles performed by Muhammad. However, most Muslims regard the Revelation of the QUR'AN as the great miracle manifested through the Prophet. In recent centuries, Muslim modernists have tried to play down the vast body of traditional miracle literature associated with Muhammad, but the miracle stories still function to inspire the faithful. The orthodox position is that prophets, including Muhammad, have no power to perform miracles of themselves but rather that God performs miracles in their name. The *Qur'an* mentions only three miraculous events and they are celebrated in Muslim life: the Night Journey, the Splitting of the Moon and the Opening of the Breast. (*See also* KARAMA; MI'RAJ)

**Mujtahid**    Someone versed in grammatical, legal and theological training and considered qualified to carry out IJTIHAD, or independent reasoning or initiative to understand the right action or correct interpretation of the QUR'AN or HADITH. The mediaeval ULAMA declared the door of *ijtihad* closed but several prominent Muslim scholars through to the present day have announced themselves as *mujtahid* including most of the leaders of the twentieth-century revival movements. (*See also* IJMA)

**Mulk**    A form of ownership in Islamic law approximately corresponding to modern freehold.

**Mumin**    *Lit. faithful.* A term used for believers or practising Muslims who are perceived to have given themselves wholeheartedly in submission to Allah's will. They are considered to be at peace with themselves and creation. (*See also* ISLAM)

**Munafiqun**    A term used in the QUR'AN for hypocrites or those that state they are believers but do so in order to benefit politically or socially but do not really believe in the *Qur'an* and the Prophet. Muslim revivalists sometimes use it to describe nominal Muslims who claim membership of the *umma* but do not practise their religion and its obligatory duties. (*See also* MUMIN; MUSLIM; NIFAQ)

**Muraqaba**  A technique of contemplation commonly used in Sufism in which a practitioner attempts to attain spiritual communion through concentration on a verse from the QUR'AN, or visualizing the form of Muhammad or one's spiritual master. The latter very often takes place at a SUFI's tomb. (*See also* DHIKR; MAZAR; TARIQA; WALI)

**Murid**  A follower or disciple of a SUFI master. The Sufi TARIQAS (paths) are based upon the relationship between the MURSHID (spiritual director) and the MURID (aspirant). The aspirant is expected to travel in search of a master. Once found, the aspirant takes BAI'A or initiation at the hands of the master. Many prominent Sufis have had several masters before arriving at their final one. (*See also* SHAIKH)

**Murji'ite**  An early group of Muslim theologians who believed in 'postponement' or leaving punishment or rewards to Allah at the Last Day. They were opposed to the more extreme of the KHARIJITES who considered that it was right to proclaim JIHAD against unjust Muslim rulers. The basic premise of the Murji'ites is that possession of faith is sufficient over deeds in order to be defined as a Muslim. The political implications were that bad rulers had to be obeyed as they ruled by God's will. (*See also* MU'TAZILA)

**Murshid**  A Sufi master or teacher (*See also* PIR; SHAIKH)

**Musa**  The Muslim name for Moses, the prophet of Allah to whom the book known as the TAWRAH was given. Moses is regarded as the prophet who brought the Revelation to the Jewish people. Their disobedience led to the coming of Jesus whose mission was to restore the inner dimension to the Jewish law and try for the last time to guide the Jewish people to the correct observance of the *Tawrah*. The final Revelation given to Muhammad gave the responsibility to the Arab nation but was a universal message for all humanity. (*See also* AHL-AL-KITAB; MUHAMMAD; NABI; RASUL)

**Musafaha**   The joining of hands between an adherent and a SUFI master which affirms discipleship and formalizes the relationship of MURID and MURSHID. The handclasping takes place in the initiation ceremony known as BAI'A. (*See also* PIR; SHAIKH)

**Mushriq**   *Lit. an idolater.* The worst offence in Islam, which espouses a rigorous and strict polytheism. The term applies to someone who worships other gods alongside Allah. This person is guilty of SHIRK, the gravest sin. Christians are sometimes referred to in this way for their maintenance of the doctrine of the Trinity and some Muslim groups have accused other Muslims of veering towards idolatry in their respect and veneration of Muhammad. Maulana MAWDUDI accused of this sin Muslims who paid loyalty to human political systems that acknowledged the sovereignty of the people rather than the sovereignty of Allah.

**Muslim (m) / Muslima (f)**   A practitioner of Islam or one who submits to Allah through obedience to the Revelation and belongs to the community of Islam. It is used to describe both those who have been born into the faith and those who have converted. The minimum requirement to become a Muslim is the uttering of the SHAHADAH in front of two witnesses. But there has been division of the community in regard to defining a Muslim. Some groups, notably the KHARIJITES and some contemporary revivalist movements have attempted to define Muslim according to practice rather than birth. The traditional position is to suspend judgment as only Allah can know the depths of the human heart. (*See also* ISLAM; MUMIN)

**Mustafa**   *Lit. 'the chosen one'.* A name given to Muhammad that refers to his role as the seal of the prophets and the vehicle for Allah's final Revelation. (*See also* MUHAMMAD)

**Mutakullum (Urdu)**   A Muslim speaker or preacher who may attend the JUMA prayers or a variety of public festivals or religious conferences. (*See also* IMAM; KHATIB; ULEMA)

**Mu'tazila**   *Lit. the neutralists.* A group of MURJI'TES who maintained neutrality in the political divisions between ALI and his opponents as they advocated a strict predeterminism that allowed for no human free will. This became a pure determinism that accepted moral laxity on the grounds that everything is predetermined and it could therefore be used politically to justify corrupt regimes, leading to a conservatism that forbade changing the status quo.

**Muzdalifah** The place where the pilgrims on the HAJJ pass the night in the open after the ninth day of the pilgrimage which is spent standing from noon to sunset listening to sermons on ARAFAT, thirteen miles from MAKKAH.

**Nabi**   One of the many prophets or messengers of Allah, usually used to refer to a messenger who does not receive a revelation in the form of a Book and is chosen to warn human beings of the consequences of disobedience to God's commandments and the rewards of obedience. Although the QUR'AN focuses on the Jewish prophets, it acknowledges that there have been thousands of such prophets across all cultures. Those that come with a Book of Revelation are much more uncommon. (*See also* RASUL)

**Nadhir**   A term that describes one of the essential activities of a prophet and refers to his role in warning of the penalties of disobedience to God's commandments and the risks of relying on anything that is not God. All prophets, whether their status is NABI or RASUL, perform the function of warning.

**Nafs**   A term used in Sufism and traditional Islam to describe the lower self, egocentricity or the base instincts and evil qualities which need to be overcome, subdued and transformed or dissolved by purification – arrived at by remembering Allah through DHIKR, prayer, reciting the QUR'AN or any other of the requirements of Islam. Muhammad described the battle to purify the *nafs* as the greater JIHAD and beholden on every Muslim. (*See also* QALB; SUFI)

**Najdites**   A sect of KHARIJITES who came to dominate Arabia until defeated by the UMAYYADS. They were more moderate in regard to their position on expulsion from the community than other Kharijite movements. This was probably because they had to moderate the extreme positions often associated with the movement in order to regulate territory.

**Namaz (Urdu)**   Used by Muslims in the Indian subcontinent as a name for SALAH or the five-times-daily obligatory prayers.

**Naqshbandi / Naqshbandiya**   The largest of the SUFI orders and the most orthodox in their attitude to the SHARI'A. They are found throughout the Muslim world but came from three original lines that developed in India, Central Asia and Turkey. The original founder was Baha'ud'din an-Naqshbandi (d. 1389). He traced his own lineage back to Muhammad, but uniquely amongst the Sufi orders, it comes up through ABU BAKR rather than ALI. The Naqshbandi are famous for performing their DHIKR (remembrance of Allah) in silence, although it is rare to find the pure silent form today. The Naqshbandi were prominent in reforming and reviving Islam in the eighteenth and nineteenth centuries and remain active and influential in contemporary Muslim societies. (*See also* SILSILA; TARIQA)

**Nasik**   A term used for some of the pious Muslims in the early period after the death of Muhammad who lived in AL-MADINAH and maintained a life of humility, simplicity and asceticism based on the model of the Prophet rather than being caught up in the perceived worldliness and luxury of the UMAYYAD empire. They are sometimes seen as the forerunners of the SUFIS.

**Na't (Urdu)**   A song of praise in honour of Muhammad and traditionally sung in the MOSQUE at the end of Friday prayers. There are many such prayers to the Prophet and they provide excellent examples of Muslim piety and the importance of the relationship with God's chosen final Prophet. They speak of the Prophet's compassion, humility, wisdom and special closeness to God. (*See also* MUHAMMAD; NUR I MUHAMMAD)

**Nifaq**   One of the great sins, and a term for hypocrisy or pretended belief in the QUR'AN which is devoid of real faith. The condition of hypocrisy is much criticized in the *Qur'an*. (*See also* MUNAFIQUN)

**Niyyah** *Lit. intention.* The statement of intent which must precede all ritual acts in Islam. Before WUDU, the ritual bathing, a Muslim repeats, 'I make the ritual intention of legal purification.' When standing to perform prayer, again a similar formula is followed: 'I stand facing the QIBLA, and raising my hands to the level of my ears, I say: "I make my intention to perform the two prostrations of the prescribed prayer-rite."' There is also a tradition that extends the *niyyah* to the condition of the Muslim's heart as he walks to the MOSQUE. The idea of *niyyah* is to ensure that the heart is engaged in religious practice and that the worshipper is not merely going through the motions. (*See also* SALAH)

**Noor (Urdu)** *See* NUR.

**Noor e Muhammadi (Urdu)** *See* NUR I MUHAMMADI.

**Nubuwwa** The concept of the pre-eternal lamp of prophethood that is exemplified and perfectly manifested in Muhammad as opposed to the physical appearance of the prophethood as manifested in the historical figure of the final Prophet. (*See also* NUR I MUHAMMADI; RISALA)

**Nur / Noor (Urdu)** The primordial light of Allah. (*See also* NUR I MUHAMMADI)

**Nur i Muhammadi / Noor e Muhammadi (Urdu)** A SUFI and SHI'A doctrine which acknowledges that Muhammad has a primordial existence as an emanation of God's light which pre-existed creation. This primordial pre-creation light from which all prophets, angels, saints and ordinary human beings were created, passed down unimpaired into the final Prophet. The Shi'a believe that this process continues into the direct bloodline through ALI and FATIMA and down through the Imamate. (*See also* BASHAR; MUHAMMAD; NUBAWWA)

**Ottoman**   The Ottoman empire was built upon the Mongol–Turkish inheritance of Genghis Khan and his successors. In 1453, Mehmet II resided over the fall of Constantinople and the old Christian Byzantine empire. He established his capital Istanbul on the old site of Constantinople and provided a major Muslim force on the borders of Europe and Asia. The Ottomans combined a warrior tradition with Islam's message of universal conversion and religious struggle. At their peak the empire extended throughout the Middle East, North Africa and into eastern Europe. After two centuries of struggle with a threatened Europe they were finally stopped at the Battle of Lepanto in 1571. By the 1600s, the Ottoman empire was at its peak. Istanbul had a population of over half a million and was an international centre of Muslim culture. The empire finally came to an end after the First World War when it broke up and Turkey emerged as a new nation. (*See also* MOGUL; SAFAVID)

**Paasban (Urdu)**　A social-work programme developed by Islamic revivalist movements such as JAMAAT-I ISLAMI that reflects their ideology that there is no differentiation between religion and politics in Islam. As their overriding goal is the establishment of an Islamic state, they are also registered as political parties. Increasingly they have organized themselves into productive welfare movements.

**Pir (Urdu)**　The term used on the Indian subcontinent for a Muslim saint or a SUFI teacher; also used in Iran and Turkey. It is the equivalent of the title 'SHAIKH' used throughout the rest of the Arab-speaking Muslim world. (*See also* PIRBHAI)

**Pirbhai (Urdu)**　A term used on the Indian subcontinent for a fellow-follower of a PIR or co-members of a SUFI TARIQA. The influence of Sufism is so great in certain parts of India, such as the Punjab, that to be described as *be-pir* (without a *pir*) is tantamount to describing someone as godless.

**Pirzada / Pirzade (Urdu)**　*See* SAJJADA NASHIN.

**Purdah**　The term used generally to describe the veiling and seclusion of women. Usually, the women of the family will have their own quarters in the household and will not appear before men who are not close relatives. They are not required to attend the MOSQUE for prayer but may pray at home. The degree of *purdah* will vary from culture to culture and household to household. Traditionally Muslim women found a greater degree of *purdah* in the cities as village life necessitated that they performed an economic role in the fields. Often middle-class urban men would demonstrate their own status by maintaining strict *purdah* on their womenfolk. However, this is increasingly under pressure from the changing economic situations in many Muslim nations where women are entering paid employment. (*See also* HIJAB)

**Qadar** The total control of Allah over destiny, or the fulfilment of events which provides Islam with a strong sense of predestination. There were several debates in the first two centuries of Muslim history in regard to the relationship between free will and predestination. These were finally resolved by al-ASHARI. (*See also* QADARITES)

**Qadarites** An early theological group that maintained that human beings had control over their own destinies and the power to determine events. The Qadarite justification for their position was that since Allah had dispensed rewards and punishments for human actions, God became a tyrant if He then totally controlled all these actions. The counter-arguments revolved around God's omniscience. The ASHARITE position of compromise eventually became orthodoxy. (*See also* KALAM)

**Qadi** The title of a Muslim judge who administers the SHARI'A or Islamic law. The ideal of the Qadi is of a man who is qualified in Muslim law but also pious in religious devotion. Islamic law states that he must treat all citizens equally and they all must have the right of a personal appearance before him. All defendants have the privilege to take an oath and the Qadi has an obligation to dispense *Hadd* (deterrent) punishments if the crime is definitely proved without a shadow of a doubt.

**Qadiriya / Qadiriyya** A SUFI order believed to have been founded by Abdul Qadir GILANI and passed on through his sons. However, the

TARIQA (order) never achieved the universal acclaim given to its founder by all Sufis throughout the Muslim world. In many areas it remained a small local order, spreading relatively late into India (sixteenth century) and Turkey (seventeenth century). Some Western scholars have cast doubt on whether Abdul Qadir Gilani was a Sufi at all and point out that he was an orthodox HANBALI ALIM who did not introduce anything innovatory into Muslim life. Even Muslim commentators point out that he was known for his orthodoxy, sermons and courses on religious instruction but did not promote Sufi teachings. However, there is no doubt that after his death he grew to become known as the foremost of all Sufis and the *tariqa* is proud to be associated with him as its founder.

**Qalandari**   A type of Sufism often associated with wandering FAQIRS who have little contact with the established TARIQAS where disciples gather around a teacher (SHAIKH). Qalandaris may have received initiation from a *shaikh* but pass their lives moving from place to place often maintaining celibacy. Their spiritual focus is on the inner experience of the ecstatic heart and they often reject both social norms and the outer observances of Islam such as prayer and fasting. (*See also* SUFI)

**Qalb**   The heart or the spiritual centre of human beings where God can be perceived. In SUFI theosophy, the heart is made unclean by the activities of the NAFS. The most common metaphor for the heart is the mirror. A dirty mirror cannot reflect the Truth but the heart purified by the unbroken remembrance of Allah becomes a clear mirror which reflects the Face of the Divine Beloved. (*See also* DHIKR)

**Qari'ah**   The preaching of the last day or the Day of Judgment that is so prominent in the early revelations of the QUR'AN. The MAKKAN Revelations seem to suggest that such a day is close. It is described as the Day of Separation, the Day of the Reckoning, the Calamity, the Smiting. Muslims do not believe that it is possible for anyone to know when the time will come but it is a terrible summons that will usher the final retribution of God upon the sins of the human race.

**Qawwali (Urdu)** A form of devotional singing in veneration of Muhammad, ALI and some famous SUFI masters popular in the Indian subcontinent. The singing is associated with the CHISHTIYA Sufi order, the largest in the subcontinent, and believed to have been introduced by their founder Mu'inuddin CHISHTI as a means to promote Islam to the Hindu population when he realized how much they used music in their religious life. The *qawwalis* are used as the main form of DHIKR (remembrance of Allah) by followers of the order and large gatherings can generate considerable fervour. *Qawwali* music has been popularized by professional musicians, such as Nusrat Fateh Ali Khan, to an international audience belonging to all religious communities.

**Qibla / Qiblah** The direction which all Muslims face when in prayer. The QIBLA marks the axis towards the KA'ABA in MAKKAH and every MOSQUE must contain a niche to indicate the right direction for Muslims to face. Kenneth Cragg has described Muslims as 'the People of the Point' in that the focus of all the various communities around the world is on one geographical point. (*See also* MIHRAB)

**Qiyas** A legal principle introduced by ABU HANIFA to deduce the correct interpretation of Islamic law by the process of applying the QUR'AN and the HADITH to new situations by the use of analogical deduction. Although the *Qur'an* may not, for example, mention travel by car, certain laws may be developed by looking at what the text says about travel utilizing the means available at the time and then employing a deductive process to arrive at a *Qur'anic* interpretation of the new situation. (*See also* IJMA; IJTIHAD; RA'Y; SHARI'A)

**Qur'an** The final Revelation of Allah to humanity and believed to be God's speech or the Word of God. Muslims believe that since the *Qur'an* is God's own words to humanity, it must also be eternal, as anything associated with God must exist for eternity. Although other revelations were given to Christians and Jews, it is believed that they corrupted their holy books. But Muslims believe that the *Qur'an* has been kept in the pure form revealed to Muhammad by the angel JIBRIL and recited by him to the first Muslims. It was collected by them and transcribed to become the sacred book of Islam at the time of the third

Caliph UMAR. As the book is literally the speech of God, it is not only the meaning which is important. The actual Arabic words are imbued with sacredness and potency and will give blessings if recited even if the reciter does not understand them. The recitation is so important that all MOSQUES will train young boys to remember parts of the *Qur'an* by rote. The most successful go on to remember by heart all of the text and are called upon to perform recitals at various public occasions. (*See also* AHL AL-KITAB; KITAB)

**Quraysh / Quraish**   The ruling clan or tribe in MAKKAH at the time of the Prophet who had benefited from the new-found merchant wealth and derived considerable income from the pilgrims who came to worship the idols installed in the KA'ABA. Muhammad was a lesser member of the tribe but they opposed his message of monotheism as they thought it would impact on their incomes. Although defeated and discredited by the success of the Muslims, they were able to re-establish their position in Arab society after his death. They became one of the forces that influenced the political dynamics of the new Arab empire and after the death of ALI, the fourth Caliph, re-emerged as the leaders of the UMAYYAD dynasty under MU'AWIYYA.

**Qush**   The missionary tours undertaken by the international proselytizing movement known as TABLIGH-I JAMAAT which was founded by Muhammad Ilyas in India. Volunteers influenced by the movement offer up to six months in a year to join preaching tours where they work with a party and target a particular Muslim area. The group will stay in the local MOSQUE and preach. Members of the group will go from house to house, encouraging the occupiers to attend the mosque and join the prayers. The movement preaches a simple message of a return to prayer and obedience to the basics of Islam infused with strong piety.

**Qutb**   *Lit. axis.* In the theosophy of Sufism, the head of an invisible hierarchy of saints upon whom the order of the universe depends. The imperative mood of direct mystical knowledge of God leads to the belief that the Qutb periodically manifests to a chosen group of elite mystics and directs the activities of all the WALI (SUFI masters) both alive and dead. This ideal of a master of masters in the mystical tradition, who corresponds to the role of Muhammad as the ultimate and final Prophet, goes back in Muslim history at least to the ninth century. Ibn ARABI wrote the most developed theosophy of the Qutb. It is generally accepted by most Sufi orders that Abdul Qadir GILANI was a manifestation of the Qutb, but rivalry between the orders often leads disciples to proclaim their own master as possessing such illustrious credentials. (*See also* SHAIKH)

**Qutb, Sayyid**   Sayyid Qutb was the successor to Hasan AL BANNA, after his death in 1949, as the new leader of the IKHWAN AL-MUSLIMUN (Islamic Brotherhood) in Egypt. Sayyid Qutb was executed in 1965 for political activities affirming the need for an Islamic state in Egypt as opposed to the modern nation state. Sayyid Qutb's ideas are very similar to those of Mawlana MAUDUDI of the Indian subcontinent. (*See also* JAMAAT-I ISLAMI)

**Qutbah**   *See* KHUTBA.

# R

**Rabi'a**  *See* AL-ADAWIYA.

**Rahma li-l'alamin**  *Lit. a mercy to the worlds.* The QUR'AN's description of Muhammad which provides Muslims with the special sense that Muhammad is unique amongst the messengers of God and opens up the possibility of veneration and piety directed towards the Prophet that has always been the hallmark of traditional Islam. (*See also* MUHAMMAD; RASUL; USWA HASANA)

**Rak'ah**  A unit of the obligatory prayer or SALAH which is made up of a set ritual recitation, standing, bowing and two prostrations. A minimum number of *rak'ahs* is required to complete the communal prayer but individuals may perform extra units both before and after that event.

**Ramadan / Ramazan (Urdu)**  The ninth month of the Muslim year which is observed as a fast lasting from sunrise to sunset. The fast is one of the five pillars of Islam and during this period Muslims should abstain from food, water and sexual activity. The fast is commanded by Allah in the QUR'AN and is therefore obligatory for all adult Muslims except in special circumstances such as illness or menstruation. In such circumstances it is permissible to make up the period of the fast at a later date. The period of Ramadan includes some of the holiest occasions of the Muslim year such as the Night of Power that marks the first revelation of the *Qur'an* to Muhammad. The fast ends with the festival of ID AL-FITR. The month of Ramadan is a period of extra religious sensitivity and many Muslims who are not usually observant will attend the MOSQUE and perform their prayers five times a day. The fast provides an opportunity to reflect on religious matters and pass a month in prayer but is also considered to be a means of creating empathy for the poor and needy in the community. (*See also* ITIKAF; LAYLAT-UL-QADR)

**Rashidun**   *See* AL-KHALIFA-UR-RASHIDUN.

**Rasul**   A prophet or messenger of Allah who is sent with a Book of Revelation. The QUR'AN acknowledges that there are thousands of messengers from God to all human cultures but there are a much smaller number who are blessed to receive God's Revelation that contains the detailed commandments of how to live a life of submission and obedience. This Revelation is given in the form of a Holy Book that contains the specifics of how to live a life of closeness to God through obedience. The chosen human vehicle to receive the Revelation, live an exemplary life based on its tenets, and preach its message to others is the *rasul*. Most prominent amongst these are IBRAHIM, Moses, David, Jesus and the final messenger, Muhammad. (*See also* DIN; NABI; NADHIR; RISALA; SHARI'A; WAHY)

**Ra'y**   The process of utilizing expert private opinion in interpreting the QUR'AN and SUNNA of the Prophet in order to form jurisprudence. There has been considerable debate as to the freedom of scholars and the limitations that need to be imposed on such activity. (*See also* FIQH; IJMA; IJTIHAD; QIYAS)

**Riba**   The Muslim understanding of usury which is forbidden in the QUR'AN. Muslim law generally interprets this to mean the making of gain without due return. Thus a distinction is made between usury and profit. The legitimate return for wealth is usually perceived to be that where the investor is personally involved in the enterprise and does not seek a guaranteed return for investment. Thus, for example, Muslims should not invest on stock exchanges where investors are not involved in the enterprises that make use of their capital.

**Rida**   The state of grace in which a person is able to say from the deepest part of the heart that he / she finds satisfaction only in God. This deep satisfaction has been a hallmark of Muslim piety and manifested amongst the countless WALIS or friends of God usually known as SUFIS. In this state of being whatever manifests is the will of God and is therefore accepted and embraced. (*See also* ISLAM)

**Risala / Risalah**   The Office of the Prophethood. (*See also* RASUL)

**Rumi, Jalalu'din**   (1207–73) A famous mystic and SUFI who founded the MAWLAWI order commonly known as the 'whirling dervishes'. Originally from Balkh in modern Afghanistan, Rumi's family settled in Konya, now in Turkey, escaping from wars and disturbance. His father was a Sufi whose teachings were accepted in Konya. It is said that Rumi himself was a great scholar of Muslim jurisprudence but may have studied Sufism under al-Tirmidhi. However, it was Rumi's meeting with the wandering FAQIR, Shams al-Tabriz, that completely transformed his life. The love between the two has become the exemplar of the relationship between disciple and master. After his master's tragic death, Rumi continued to attract disciples and the city of Konya became famous as the centre of the growing Sufi order. Rumi was known for his ecstatic movement to celebrate his experience of Allah and it was this that developed into the unique practice of the Mawlawi TARIQA. Rumi's magnificent collection of his experience written as poetry and called the MATHNAWI is famous throughout the Muslim world but especially in Persia where it is known as a spiritual commentary on the QUR'AN.

**S**

**Sabr**  The spiritual quality of patience and fortitude in adversity that leads to endurance. In Muslim spirituality, this state of being develops through trust in God and the knowledge that everything, even adversity, is Allah's inscrutable will. It is expressed in the phrase, *Al-hamdu lillahi 'ala kulli hal*, or, praise be to God under all conditions. (*See also* HAMD)

**Sadaqah**  A good deed or voluntary payment of charity that is independent and extra to the obligatory payment of ZAKAH.

**Safa**  One of the two hills in MAKKAH which are now inside the precincts of the Grand MOSQUE. The two hills (MARWAH and Safa) are said to be the location of HAJAR's desperate search for water in order to save her child ISHMAEL from dying of thirst. She ran back and forth between the two hills pleading for God's mercy and intervention. The miraculous appearance of the ZAMZAM spring not only saved Hajar and Ishmael but also ensured Makkah's location as a place for caravans to stop on route through the desert. The pilgrims on the annual HAJJ reenact Hajar's desperation by running back and forth between the two hills.

**Safavid**  The Safavid dynasty or empire in Persia lasted from 1501 to 1722. The Safavids began as a revivalist SUFI order in the thirteenth century but were transformed by the time that they came to power in a religio-political movement combining SHI'A doctrines of the messianic return of the IMAM and a call for armed struggle against other Muslim regimes. In 1501, Ishmael, who claimed to be a descendant of the Shi'a

Imams, conquered Tabriz and declared himself the Shah of Iran. He built an empire comprising of modern day Iran to the east of the Ottomans. In doing so, he declared Shi'a Islam the official religion of his empire. The Shah considered himself to be both a religious and temporal leader, both emperor and messianic messenger. The Shahs ruled as 'Shadow of God on Earth' and all other religious beliefs were suppressed. The Sufi past of Iran with its veneration of saints was exchanged for the key figures in the Shi'a past such as the family of ALI and the Imams. The Safavid empire reached its peak under Shah Abbas (1588–1629) who embarked upon an ambitious programme of state building including a major building programme supported by endowments. (*See also* MOGUL; OTTOMAN)

**Sahaba**   The Companions of the Prophet Muhammad who became the first Muslims and his loyal and devoted followers. The Sahaba not only provide a role model for Muslim piety but are also important for ensuring the authenticity of accounts of Muhammad's words and deeds as transmitted through the HADITH. Each *hadith* must have a chain of transmission that goes back to one of the Companions in order to be considered authentic. (*See also* ISNAD)

**Sahih al-Bukhari**   The title of the collection of HADITH compiled by Muhammad Ibn Ishmael al-BUKHARI (810–70). This is one of the six collections of Muhammad's deeds and sayings described as authentic or reliable. Al-Bukhari's collection of over seven thousand *hadith* is regarded as next only to the QUR'AN in authority. In some places, the whole of Bukhari's *Sahih* was read out publicly during the month of RAMADAN.

**Sahih Muslim**   The title of the collection of HADITH compiled by Abul Husayn Muslim ibn al-Hajjaj (d. 875). This is one of the six collections of *hadith* described as authentic or reliable. It is considered to be second only to the collection compiled by al-BUKHARI.

**Sahir**   Evil sorcerers or magicians who seek the assistance of demons or bad spirits to acquire special powers as opposed to the MU'AZZIMUN who seek the help of God to exorcise JINN possession.

**Saiyid**   *See* SAYYID.

**Sajjada nashin (Urdu)**   *Lit. he who sits on the mat.* The term used to describe the ancestral successors to a PIR or saint from the SUFI tradition. Many traditional Muslims believe that the bloodline endows the descendents of a holy man with innate spirituality. Very often, the *sajjada nashin* will function as the hereditary leaders of the saint's order and custodians of his tomb and shrine. (*See also* DARGAH; MAZAR; SILSILA; TARIQA)

**Salaam**   *See* AS-SALAMU-ALAYKUM.

**Salafi**   The movement founded by Muhammad ABDUH (d. 1905) which influenced nationalist groups in North Africa and was essentially a group of back-to-basics or fundamentalist reformers opposed to traditional Islam, especially Sufism. The Salafi view of Muhammad is essentially influenced by rational and humanitarian ideals meeting the Muslim world from Europe in the nineteenth and twentieth centuries. The Prophet is regarded as a founder of a virtuous community and a moral leader who transformed Arab society, but the mystical and devotional emphasis of the mediaeval period is criticized. In the late twentieth century, new forms of Salafi thinking have developed with a much more aggressive stance towards traditional Muslims and the West. (*See also* MUHAMMAD; SUFI)

**Salah / Salat**   The second pillar of Islam or the five-times-daily prayer as believed by Muslims to be prescribed by Allah as the correct form of worship. Western scholars note that the prayer-rite is not mentioned in the QUR'AN and was gradually developed by Muslims. However, Muslim commentators are clear that the distinctive movements and recitals were used by Muhammad and passed on to his companions. The movement consists of three positions: standing, bowing and prostrating. The whole sequence of three positions and the words repeated is known as a RAK'AH. Each one of the five prayer occasions may contain several *rak'ahs*, although two is the minimum when praying formally behind the IMAM. Worshippers can perform individual prayers both before and after the formal prayer. The prayers follow the ADHAN or prayer-call traditionally made from the MINARET of the MOSQUE and Muslims are required to ritually wash before the prayer (WUDU). When the prayer begins, the congregation stands in lines or rows, shoulder to shoulder. The five occasions of prayer are as follows: *Salat ul-Fajr* performed between dawn and sunrise; *Salat ul-Zuhr* performed immediately after noon; *Salat ul-Asr* performed in the late afternoon; *Salat ul-Maghrib* performed immediately after sunset; *Salat ul-Isha* performed in the night but not later than midnight. There are also two optional prayers performed by Muhammad and very devout Muslims. These are *Salat al-Lail*, performed in the night between midnight and dawn; and *Salat al-Duha*, performed between dawn and the noon prayer. (*See also* ASR; FAJR; ISHA; MAGHRIB; ZUHR)

**Salawat sharifa**    Countless formulas that bless Muhammad and his family and known as *darud-i sharif* in the subcontinent. These are particularly emphasized by the SUFI tradition but millions of traditional Muslims sing or chant them, sometimes after morning and sunset prayers. Many are used as intercessionary prayers and it is generally believed that intercession is not possible without first calling blessings upon the Prophet. The most common form of blessing is *salla Allahu alaihi wa sallam* (God bless him and give him peace) which is uttered every time a pious Muslim mentions the Prophet's name. (*See also* DU'A; ISTIGHATHA; SHAFA'A)

**Salik**    The second stage of SUFI discipleship known as the journeyer or pilgrim. In this context it refers not to outward pilgrimage but spiritual travelling to attain proximity to Allah. However, as a stage of progress it refers to the need for the seeker of truth to travel in search of an enlightened master or SHAIKH who can provide the guidance required to develop the seeker's innate capacity to come closer to God through purification of the heart. (*See also* NAFS; QALB; TARIQA)

**Sama**    *Lit. hearing.* The term used to describe listening to music as a spiritual discipline in some SUFI orders, notably the CHISHTI. It is also the term used for the dervish or MAWLAWI turning ceremony commonly described as a mystical dance. Early commentators describe Sufi gatherings using music and rhythmical movements to induce ecstasy. Although there has been considerable debate regarding the lawfulness of music, it is generally considered that the human voice aided by drums is permissible. (*See also* DHIKR; RUMI)

**Samad**   *Lit. eternal.* One of the ninety-nine names of Allah that describe His attributes. *Samad* is commonly chanted in DHIKR gatherings.

**Sanusi / Sanusiya / Sanusiyya**   A reform SUFI order popular in North Africa. It was founded by Muhammad ibn Ali as-Sanusi (1787–1859). The founder preached to the tribes of the Sahara a form of Sufism that focused on DHIKR but played down the emotional excesses criticized by the WAHABIS and SALAFIS. The movement succeeded through its adaptation of Sufi lodges or ZAWIYAS to the nomadic people of the desert. Each lodge contained a complex of buildings that included a MOSQUE, a school, retreat cells, guest blocks and residences for students constructed around an inner courtyard and a well. A wall that could be defended if necessary encompassed the complete structure. The surrounding land was cultivated. The *zawiya* was regarded as belonging to the tribe whose territory it inhabited. (*See also* TARIQA)

**Saum / Sawm**   Fasting and abstinence from just before dawn until sunset, performed during the month of RAMADAN. The observance of the fasting is binding on all adult Muslims save for the aged, the sick, menstruating and pregnant women, nursing mothers and travellers. However, it is expected that those who are able to observe the fast but are prevented by changeable circumstances such as travelling or menstruation should make up the period of fasting as soon as possible after the month of Ramadan.

**Sayyid / Saiyid**   A title of respect given to descendants of Muhammad, especially through his grandsons, HUSAIN and HASAN. Although the respect and veneration given to the Prophet's bloodline is universal it is emphasized in the SHI'A tradition. However, SUNNI Muslims also regard the descendents of the Prophet with respect and the SUFIS have always given their veneration to the Prophet's family. Al-Hallaj, the great Sufi mystic, declared that 'God has not created anything that is dearer to him than Muhammad and his family'. (*See also* ALI)

**Seera (Urdu)** *See* SIRA.

**Shafa'a** *Lit. intercession.* Although the countless SUFI saints are believed to be able to intercede on behalf of the petitioner to Allah, the prime intercessor for Muslims is Muhammad, the final Prophet. Millions of Muslims pray to Allah through the intercession of Muhammad and even ask for forgiveness of their sins by invoking his name as Allah's favoured beloved. It is generally believed by most Muslims that the Prophet will mediate and intercede on their behalf at the Day of Judgment. (*See also* DU'A; ISTIGHATHA; TAWASSUL)

**Shafi'i** One of the four schools of jurisprudence, named after its founder, Muhammad ibn Idris al-Shafi'i (d. 820), and centred in Cairo and Baghdad. Al-Shafi'i was instrumental in developing the principles of Islamic jurisprudence where the verbal tradition of the HADITH took precedence over customary tradition. (*See also* HANBALI; HANIFI; MALIKI)

**Shahadah** The proclamation that 'there is no god but God; and Muhammad is His prophet' (*la illaha illa'llah, Muhammadun rasulu 'llah*) which forms the basis of the Muslim confession of faith. This is the first pillar of Islam, also known as the KALIMA, and its utterance is the only requirement for becoming a Muslim. The *shahadah* is a covenant between the Muslim and Allah which opens the doors of Paradise, and Muslims hope to recite it as their last words before death. It is regarded as protection against evil and a means of forgiveness of sins. The first part of the *shahadah* is continuously repeated as a means of spiritual discipline and remembrance of God by most of the SUFI orders. (*See also* DHIKR; SHAHID; TARIQA)

**Shahid** *Lit. a witness.* Every Muslim is a witness to the oneness of Allah and finality of Muhammad as the seal of the prophets. This is testified through the SHAHADAH and the obligation to promote Islam. However, the term has become inextricably linked with martyrdom as the ultimate testimony of faith. Martyrdom should not be sought intentionally as that could be tantamount to suicide but the martyr's place in paradise is secured. It is believed that the martyr, defined as one who dies when involved in JIHAD, finds immediate rest in paradise and does not have to wait until the final Day of Judgment. (*See also* DAWA; JIHAD; SHAHADAH)

**Shaikh / Sheikh**   A title given to an old or respected man but often denoting a saint or spiritual master in the SUFI tradition. (*See also* PIR; WALI)

**Shaikh al-Hadith**   The title bestowed upon the senior teacher of HADITH in a Muslim religious school or DAR AL-ULUM. (*See also* MADRASA)

**Shaikh Farid**   (1173–1265) An ascetic SUFI saint whose tomb site is in Pakpattan, Pakistan. He is unique in that he has four of his poems included in the *Guru Granth Sahib*, the sacred book of the Sikhs, thus indicating the close affinity between the teachings of the Sufis and the North Indian Sants. Also known as Shakar Ganj, he is the master of Nizamuddin Awliya, the famous SHAIKH of the Indian CHISHTIS.

**Shaitan / Shaytan**   *Lit. rebellious, proud.* The term used for the devil who tries to lure human beings away from the path of righteousness. Shaitan is perceived as a hidden whisperer in the hearts of all human beings but is personified as a fallen angel who refused to bow to ADAM as a result of pride. He was cast out from the company of angels and swore to divert all human beings from God's ordinances in order to prove that they were unworthy of the honour of being Allah's representatives on earth. (*See also* IBLIS; KHALIFA)

**Shalwar kamis (Urdu)**   The distinctive long tunic and baggy trousers worn by both male and female Muslims in the subcontinent, especially the Punjab. Many Muslims of subcontinent origin who have settled in the West regard the Shalwar Kamis as obligatory dress when attending the MOSQUE even if they wear Western dress as everyday clothing. This has given a symbolic aspect to a mode of dress that is only customary in the subcontinent.

**Shari'a / Shari'ah**   Islamic law as based upon the Revelation laid out in the QUR'AN and SUNNA of Muhammad and interpreted by the founders of the four Muslim schools of law (HANAFI, HANBALI, SHAFI'I and MALIKI). One of the central tenets of Islam is that Allah is sovereign over everything and therefore only God has the right to determine the correct course of action for human beings. *Shari'a* indicates the path to be followed and literally means 'the way to the watering place'. Justice is central to the message of the *Qur'an* and in Muslim terms indicates actions that should be performed and those that are forbidden by Allah's ordinances. In the two hundred years following Muhammad's death, various Muslim commentators developed a comprehensive system of right and wrong actions based upon the Revelation in the *Qur'an* and the precedents set by the Prophet's deeds and actions. Local customs were thoroughly investigated insofar as they complied with the injunctions implicit in the Revelation. During this period a comprehensive system of law based on Allah's commandments was worked out and became the norm and the ideal for Muslim societies. Islamic family law, criminal justice, business and trade obligations and rules of warfare were all developed on the basis of Revelation. This gave rise to a unique form of government in which rulers were considered not to be lawmakers but custodians of divine law. Debates still rage in the Muslim world as to whether an Islamic state is the only vehicle for the correct maintenance of Islamic law. (*See also* FIQH)

**Shaytan**   *See* SHAITAN.

**Sheikh**   *See* SHAIKH.

**Shi'a / Shi'ah**   The first division amongst Muslims after the death of the Muhammad and the most important schism in Islam. The Shi'a believe in the succession of the direct descendents of Muhammad through the line of ALI rather than the Caliphate. This is known as the Imamate. The IMAMS are considered to be infallible bearers of esoteric wisdom with a direct spiritual contact with Muhammad. They are the source of authority upon which Shi'a theology rests. The tradition has a strong passion motive originating in the violent death of HUSAIN, the Prophet's grandson, at KARBALA at the hands of the ruling UMAYYAD dynasty. As a result of persecution and the passion motive, the Shi'a have developed a strong cult of martyrdom. The emphasis on living charismatic leaders has resulted in several divisions over leadership taking place amongst the Shi'a. The Twelver Shi'as who believe in the succession of twelve *imams* beginning with Ali are the dominant form of Islam in Iran and the largest Shi'a group. The next most prominent are the ISHMAELIS or Seveners. The other main group is the Zaidis but Shi'a has also given birth to non-Muslim religious movements: the Ba'hai and the Druse. (*See also* AYATOLLAHS; HASAN; ZAID)

**Shi'at Ali**   *Lit. the party of Ali. (See also* SHI'A)

**Shirk**   *Lit. association.* The sin of idolatry or regarding anything as equal to or partner to Allah. This is a serious or cardinal sin in Islam and is used for any serious deviation from the worship of one God. Christians are accused of *shirk* in that have provided Jesus with a status equal to God which is far above his role as a prophet or messenger of God. Contemporary debates concerning *shirk* have revolved around various ideologies such as democracy or socialism that are based on the sovereignty of the people rather than the sovereignty of Allah. Some Muslim groups have accused traditional Muslims, influenced by Sufism, of raising the status of Muhammad to a divine personality considered close to the Christian to view of Christ. (*See also* ISA; MUHAMMAD; SUFI; WAHABI)

**Shukr**   Gratitude or thankfulness which is the only correct response to the Divine. Islam has a strong mood of gratitude which is manifested in many of its prominent spiritual figures especially the SUFI tradition. Gratitude is considered the virtue of the purified heart and is not regarded as part of a bargain with God for answering human prayers for material well-being. It has sometimes been seen as a guarantee against loss of grace, but generally speaking it is perceived as its own reward for giving Allah His due and brings with it spiritual satisfaction, joy and a light heart. (*See also* HAMD; SABR)

**Shura**   *Lit. a council.* A consultative body of Muslims presiding over religious and worldly affairs and responsible for the maintenance of

Muslim law. It is prescribed by the QUR'AN as the model of leadership. (*See also* SHARI'A)

**Sihr**   The term used to describe magical or wondrous events which could include the healing properties of plants, conjuring or even astrological prediction. However, it is more commonly used to refer to prayers, ritual acts, or religious objects that are used to change the course of events by appealing to God, Muhammad or the intercession of a Muslim saint or to ask for their protection against misfortune. (*See also* also KIHANA)

**Silsila / Silsilah**   The sequence of SUFI masters that must reach back in an unbroken chain to Muhammad. All the *silsilahs* come through Muhammad to his son-in-law, ALI, except for the NAQSHBANDIS who trace their spiritual lineage through ABU BAKR. Each Sufi order (TARIQA) will have a *silsilah* which provides the order with legitimacy and ensures that the follower feels secure in the discipline. Through the line of SHAIKHS, the blessing of the Prophet and all the former masters is received through the living master. Most Sufi orders will recite the lineage after evening prayer or JUMA prayers held on Friday. (*See also* BAI'A; MURID)

**Sira / Sirat / Seera / Seerat**   Biographical writings concerned with the exemplary behaviour of Muhammad. The most respected and the source for all later versions were those written by Ibn Ishaq (d. 768) and Ibn Hisham (d. 830) based on early stories of Muhammad's deeds, the poems of Hassan ibn Thabit and accounts of Muhammad's military struggles with the opponents of Islam. They contain numerous legends constructed around a strong kernel of factual material. In the early twentieth century countless biographies of the Prophet were written and this renewed interest in the historical Muhammad became known as the Sirat movement. (*See also* HADITH; MUHAMMAD)

**Subhah**   A string of beads used to count the names of Allah during recitation, especially used by SUFIS when performing DHIKR but common amongst many traditional Muslims.

**Sufi**    Usually defined as Muslim mysticism, Sufism is a systemized method of bringing the practitioner into an alignment or correspondence with Allah, which is portrayed in terms of union or communion with the unity of the one God. By the end of the ninth century Sufis had developed both the doctrine and the methodology of the path to mystical union. The Sufi experience of union led to a profound understanding of the nature of Divinity and the human being, and brought about a unique understanding of TAUHID (oneness of Allah) not accessible to the orthodox who simply followed the outer teachings of Islam. The development of Sufism affirmed the need for a spiritual teacher who could guide the MURID (disciple) through various spiritual disciplines based on repetition of the names of Allah and leading through successive internal stages to purification of the heart and eventual loss of self into the unity of Allah. These lineages of masters developed into well-established orders that remain influential in contemporary Islam. In spite of criticism from several neo-revivalist movements, Sufism remains a viable force in the Muslim world and claims to represent the beliefs of the majority of traditional Muslims. (*See also* NAFS; QALB; SHAIKH; TARIQA; TASSAWUF)

**Sunna / Sunnah**    *Lit. the beaten path.* The exemplary practices, customs and traditions of the Prophet as recorded in the HADITH and SIRA and used as the model for Muslim behaviour and custom. The *Sunna* is regarded as the second authoritative source after the QUR'AN.

**Sunni**    The vast majority of Muslims who believe in the successorship of the Caliphs rather than the Imamate. They are the largest group within Islam and are the majority population in most Muslim nations with the exception of Iraq and Iran. However, there are debates within the Sunni community as to its constitution. Both traditional Muslims influenced by the teachings of the SUFIS and new revivalist movements such as the WAHABIS and the SALAFIS claim to be the genuine Sunni community to the exclusion of their opponents. (*See also* AHL AS-SUNNA WA JAMAAT; IMAM; KHALIFA; SHI'A)

**Sura / Surah**    The divisions of the QUR'AN into chapters consisting of AYAT or verses written in blank verse, each one given a title relevant to the theme covered. They are arranged in order of size rather than chronology with the longest appearing first. Various debates have taken place concerning the chronology of the *suras* as to whether they were revealed in MAKKAH or al-MADINAH. Generally speaking, the less legalistic, shorter *suras* were revealed in Makkah.

**Tabligh-i Jamaat**    An organization founded in the late 1920s by Muhammad Ilyas, a graduate of DEOBAND in Northern India. Unlike the Deoband members, Ilyas did not consider it necessary to belong to the professional ULAMA in order to reform Islam. Tabligh-i Jamaat is a grassroots movement to inspire religious renewal. There is no central administrative structure and the key activity is co-ordinated voluntary commitment to participate in preaching teams. These teams, numbering between three and ten members, go out to Muslim communities to inspire renewed commitment to prayer and MOSQUE attendance. The teams sleep in the local mosque and travel door to door to invite local Muslims to their meetings. The teams strongly emphasize humility and prayer and encourage others by example. As the teams progress, those that are inspired by them are formed into new preaching teams. In this way the circle of preachers has gradually increased throughout the Muslim world.

**Tafsir**    *Lit. explanation.* the science of interpretation or exegesis of the QUR'AN through commentary. Muslim commentators have considered that the best explanation of the *Qur'an* is contained in the *Qur'an* itself, as Allah would not have made the final Revelation obscure for human beings to comprehend. One part of the *Qur'an* will provide clarification for another part. However, one famous exegesist of the *Qur'an*, Dehlavi, noted three conditions that should be adhered to when engaging in commentary: i) every word should be explained by providing its real meaning and its roots in the Arabic language; ii) everything should be explained in the context of the revelation as a whole; iii) the interpretation should not be contrary to the under-standing of Muhammad's companions (SAHABA) who witnessed the Revelation. (*See also* HADITH)

**Tahiyya**  A greeting made in the prayer-rite in which the worshipper states: 'salutations and blessings and ascriptions of goodness belong to God. Peace be to you, O Prophet, and the mercy of God and His blessings. Peace be to us and to the righteous worshippers of God'. (*See also* AS-SALAMU-ALAYKUM; SALAH)

**Tahrif**  The doctrine that the scriptures of the Jews and Christians, although true revelations of the Divine word given to the respective prophets, Moses, David and Jesus, were corrupted or changed by later generations of followers. (*See also* AHL-I KITAB; INJIL; TAWRAH)

**Tajdid**  The idea that faithful believers periodically renew Islam in order to maintain the purity of the final Revelation. Many Muslims believe that every century sees the birth of a reformer who is sent to restore the faith and regenerate the community and prevent any drift away from the Revelation caused by human error or ignorance. Many new revivalist movements in the twentieth century have been concerned with *tajdid*: they often use it as a critique of the Muslim establishment and a call to purge Islam of foreign or cultural accretions. (*See also* ISLAH; MUJADDID)

**Talbiya**  *See* LABBAIKA.

**Tanzih**  The important concept of Allah's transcendence, which is linked to the central Muslim doctrine of TAUHID (Divine unity and uniqueness). There has been continuous debate concerning lines in the QUR'AN that describe Allah having qualities that could be allocated to created beings and seem to anthropomorphize the absolute transcendence of Allah. Generally, Muslims accept that Allah's attributes such as power, knowledge and will are equally absolute. (*See also* ALLAH; TANZIL)

**Tanzil**  The term used to describe the coming down or descent of the Revelation from Allah to Muhammad through JIBRIL, the angel. It is derived from the Arabic TANZIH (transcendent) and suggests a reaching out or descent of the almighty omniscient Allah to His human creation through the Revelation of His eternal Word. (*See also* QUR'AN; WAHY)

**Taqlid**    The principle of strict adherence to the established doctrines of the four schools of Islamic law that has been blamed by some revivalist movements for producing stagnation and petrification in the Muslim world. It is perceived to promote conservatism, traditionalism and uncritical veneration. (*See also* FIQH; IJTIHAD)

**Taqrirat al-rasul**    The preachings of Muhammad. These were collected from the recollections of his companions and contained in the HADITH collections. They form the second most authoritative source for Muslims after the Qur'an. (*See also* IJMA)

**Taqwa**    Self-protection or fear of God. A religious attitude of fear and awe arising from an overwhelming Muslim belief in an all-powerful, omnipresent God who has commanded submission to his will and who will give judgment to all on the Last Day. (*See also* ALLAH; IHSAN)

**Tariq al-Istikharat**    *Lit. the method of choices.* The Arabic term of bibliomancy, the practice of opening a book, usually the QUR'AN, at random as a form of divination or means to arrive at a decision when faced with several options. (*See also* ISTIKHARAT)

**Tariqa/Tariqah**    *Lit. the way.* A term used to describe the inner path of purification that parallels the maintenance of SHARI'A (Islamic law) and according to SUFIS constitutes the correct or complete practice of Islam. In order to follow the esoteric or inner path it is considered that a guide is necessary who has walked the path himself. The paths of individual guidance have developed into Sufi orders, some of which are international and contain millions of adherents. Some of the most famous of these schools of guidance along the Sufi path are the NAQSH-BANDIYA, QADIRIYA, MAWLAWI and ALAWIYA. Many may be regional or confined to a smaller locality. The organization is generally based around a group of followers studying under the guidance of an individual *shaikh* or master. Each *tariqa* is known for variations on the discipline used for self-purification. (*See also* DHIKR; MURID; TASSAWUF)

**Tasdiq**  The QUR'AN as confirmation of all the earlier revelations of Allah given to the previous messengers such as ADAM, Abraham, Moses, and Jesus. The QUR'AN is both a new Revelation but at the same time a repetition of the essentials contained in the earlier books. Thus Islam is both new in its inception and a continuation of God's one true religion. (*See also* DIN; NABI; RASUL; TANZIL; WAHY)

**Tasliya**  The common practice in prayer and on other occasions to call down blessings upon Muhammad. The most common form is used whenever a Muslim mentions the Prophet's name. There is also a blessing called for in the prayer-rite and in the call to prayer. (*See also* ADHAN; MUHAMMAD; SALAH)

**Tassawuf**  The preferred term for the spiritual or esoteric path of Islam commonly referred to as Sufism. It is generally used to describe the process of inner purification required in order to be a practising Muslim. The person who follows the inner path of purifying the heart through the remembrance of Allah as well as the outer forms of Islam is known as a SUFI or practitioner of *tassawuf*. (*See also* DHIKR; TARIQA; TAZKIYAT AL-NAFS)

**Tauhid / Tawhid**  The belief in the oneness and uniqueness of God. This is the central doctrine of Islam and leads to its assertion of uncompromising monotheism. TAUHID has two components: firstly it contains the idea of Allah's total uniqueness or otherness from His creation. He cannot be compared with anything that is known or created. This doctrine of absolute transcendence gave rise to many theological questions in Islam concerning free will, predestination, moral accountability, self-sufficiency and the problem of creation. This position left the Divine as essentially unknowable and inscrutable. Any apparent contradiction can only be resolved in God's knowledge of His own Being. On the other hand, there have been those who have concentrated more on the Oneness of God and the close relationship between worshipper and worshipped, creation and creator. Many Muslim mystics have explained creation in emanationist or panentheistic or even pantheistic terms and asserted the oneness of everything encompassed within Allah's being. Although arguable by QUR'ANIC exegesis, this has not sat comfortably with many orthodox theologians who have preferred to emphasize transcendence over immanence. (*See also* SUFI; TANZIH)

**Tawaf**  The practice of circumambulating the KA'ABA in MAKKAH seven times, performed by all Muslims when undertaking either the HAJJ or the UMRAH.

**Tawassul**  *Lit. seeking a means.* Any means which can be used by a Muslim to come closer to Allah and surrender to His will. Many traditional Muslims regard seeking assistance from Muhammad through his intercession as the most valuable form of *tawassul*. (*See also* DHIKR; ISTIGHATHA; SHAFA'A)

**Ta'widh / Ta'wiz**  Amulets or bracelets containing verses of the QUR'AN given to cure diseases or protect from ill-fortune. These are often given out by the descendents of famous mystics (SUFIS) who maintain their shrine centres or tombs. Some Muslims are highly opposed to the practice and see it as a folk superstition that has entered into Islam. However, it is undeniably true that countless millions of Muslims, especially in rural areas, maintain the practice. (*See also* BARAKA; MAZAR; SAJJADA NASHIN)

**Ta'wil**  A form of TAFSIR that provides an allegorical rather than literal exegesis of the QUR'AN. It results in a philosophical or mystical understanding and posits the view that the *Qur'an* has an esoteric or hidden meaning. It is the usual form of *tafsir* used by SUFIS.

**Tawrah**  The Arabic for the Torah or the book given to the Prophet MUSA (Moses) by Allah. It is one of the four sacred books revealed to a messenger containing the sacred law. The three earlier books have all been superseded by the final Revelation contained in the QUR'AN. (*See also* INJIL; ZABUR)

**Taymiyya, Taqi al-Din ibn** (1263–1328) A Muslim scholar who is frequently used as the inspiration for neo-orthodox movements in the twentieth century such as the WAHABIS and SALAFIS. However, Ibn Taymiyya was not as orthodox as these latter groups and was not as anti-SUFI as they declare him to be. He was opposed to those Sufis who flaunted obedience to Islamic law on the grounds that their personal inner experience negated the outer practices of Islam. Ibn Taymiyya demonstrated a remarkable degree of open-mindedness to all opinions and often made remarks such as 'the truth does not belong to one party exclusively but is divided among all groups'. He reinstated into Muslim theology the doctrine that human power and divine will are not mutually exclusive.

**Tazkiyat al-nafs** The term used in the QUR'AN to describe the process of inner purification or struggle against the ego, the part of the human psyche that refuses to submit to Allah. (*See also* NAFS; QALB; TASSAWUF)

**Uhud**   A famous battle fought in 625 by Muhammad and the first Muslims of MAKKAH and al-MADINAH against their opponents in Makkah. The battle came after the famous victory at BADR but the result almost went against the Muslims. It has been attributed to loss of discipline, and the QUR'AN rebuked the Muslims for loss of faith, stating that their near defeat was a chastisement from God. The Battle of Uhud seriously challenged the doctrine of Manifest Success confirmed at Badr. In a sense the two battles set the pattern of Muslim history. Worldly or political success is seen as a sign of Allah's favour but failure needs to be explained as a loss of faith arising in Divine displeasure. Consequently Muslims have responded to political decline with religious revival.

**Ulama / Ulema**   Religious scholars of Islamic law and jurisprudence who have graduated from a MADRASA. In the first centuries of Islam, the *ulama* created and controlled the system of education and developed the curricula to realize their own spiritual and intellectual goals. Through this they were successful in bringing a stability and cohesiveness to the community reinforced by dogmatic theology and an all-embracing legal system. In recent history, however, the *ulama* have been blamed for stifling creativity and holding to a mediaeval mindset that has blocked the development of the Muslim world. Many of the new revivalist movements in Islam with their powerful political agendas are anti-*ulama*. (*See also* FIQH; IKHWAN AL-MUSLIMUN; JAMAAT-I ISLAM; SHARI'A)

**Umam**   Plural of UMMA.

**Umar ibn ul-Khattab**   The second Caliph of Islam from 634–44 and known as one of the four righteously guided Caliphs and a father-in-law of Muhammad. During Umar's rule, the Arabs significantly expanded outwards and conquered Jerusalem. The new territories were administered effectively and the tax system helped create the wealth that provided for the extensive expansion at the time of the UMAYYADS. Muslims know Umar as a man of great piety as well as an able ruler, and countless stories are told of his wisdom and humility. (*See also* ABU BAKR; ALI; AL-KHULIFA UR-RASHIDUN; UTHMAN)

**Umayyad / Ummayad**   The first Arab Muslim dynasty founded in 661 after the death of the fourth righteously guided Caliph, ALI. The UMAYYAD dynasty was founded by MU'AWIYA who moved the capital of the new Arab empire from al-MADINAH to his own stronghold in Damascus. There are questions concerning the Umayyad's conviction towards Islam. They maintained the Caliphal form of rule and accepted the SHARI'A law as the basis of the constitution, but most of the Caliphs lived in moral laxity and the Arab state was used as foundation for the pursuit of personal power. The religious leadership remained in al-Madinah, deeply dissatisfied with the condition of the empire. Instead they focused on personal piety and the study of religious sciences such as HADITH and law. The Umayyad dynasty was superseded by the ABBASIDS in 750. (*See also* KHARIJITES; SHI'A)

**Umm al-Kitab**   The primordial prototype of the QUR'AN that pre-existed the Revelation to Muhammad. In early Muslim history, various groups disputed whether the *Qur'an* was eternal. The eventual decision was made that the *Qur'an* must have pre-existed with Allah, as it was the prototype of Revelation and the ultimate form of God's Word.

**Umma / Ummah**   The universal community of Muslims that incorporates the totality of all who profess the faith regardless of nationality, ethnicity, class or gender. It is the only community to which a Muslim belongs simply by virtue of being a Muslim. The ideal of the *umma* is of a community bound together in the beliefs and practices of

Islam, to worship Allah through submission to the Revelation conveyed to humanity through the Prophet Muhammad. The purpose of the *umma* is to act as a witness for Allah through the example of obedient worship and through the relation of one member to another. The *umma* is the ideal organization responsible for upholding the true faith and instructing humanity in the revealed way of God as contained in the QUR'AN and the SUNNA of the Prophet. Despite the ideal, held by many Muslims, of a single, Divinely revealed and united Islam, there have been and continue to be diverse interpretations of the religion and considerable challenges from nationalism, ethnicity and secularism. It is debatable whether the ideal of the *umma* has ever actually existed in reality after Muhammad's death except as a powerful symbol of cohesion. (*See also* KITAB; RASUL; SHARI'A)

**Ummah Wusta**  The ideal or model Muslim community that, according to the QUR'AN, replaces the Jewish and Christian communities that had lost their way and corrupted their revelations. Throughout Muslim history various religious factions were to declare themselves as the model Muslim community within the wider context of Muslim society. (*See also* AHL-I-KITAB; JAMAAT; UMMA)

**Ummi**  *Lit. unlettered.* The important doctrine that Muhammad was not able to read or write. Although some Western orientalists have challenged the idea that a merchant would have been illiterate, the belief is important to Muslims as it supports the idea that Muhammad could not have been the author of the QUR'AN and assists in proclaiming the miracle of the Book as the literal word of Allah. (*See also* MUHAMMAD)

**Umrah**  The lesser pilgrimage to MAKKAH which Muslims can perform at any time of the year, as opposed to the HAJJ which must be performed in the correct month.

**Urf**  Customary law or known practices of a society that are recognized by all the schools of Islamic Law as long as they do not contradict the QUR'AN or the SUNNA of the Prophet. If there is contradiction then they are outside Islamic law and forbidden to Muslims in that society. The ability to combine SHARI'A with *urf* has given Muslim society a great deal of flexibility as it has moved around the world through conquest or migration.

**Urs** *Lit. wedding.* An anniversary of a WALI's death which is regarded as celebrating their union with God. All SUFI TARIQAS will maintain an *urs* to the founder of their order and it will feature as one of the main celebrations of the liturgical year. Some *urs* celebrations in the Indian subcontinent can attract millions of pilgrims to the saint's shrine. (*See also* DARGAH; MAZAR)

**Uswa hasana** *Lit. the beautiful model.* The description of Muhammad as the ideal embodiment of the *Qur'anic* revelation and the exemplar for all Muslims to follow. The QUR'AN states: *to obey him is to obey God* (4:80). For this reason the *sunna* of the Prophet sits next to the *Qur'an* as a source of inspiration and direction for Muslims. (*See also* ADAB; MUHAMMAD)

**Uthman** The third Caliph of Islam from 644–56 and known as one of the four righteously guided Caliphs and a companion of Muhammad. Uthman compiled the authoritative version of the QUR'AN and ordered the destruction of alternative versions. Uthman was an old man by the time that he inherited the Caliphate and it is debatable whether he had the ability to rule the expanding empire with the expertise of ABU BAKR and UMAR. Charges of nepotism were widespread. In June 656 he was assassinated by the son of Abu Bakr and a group of insurgents who had been part of an uprising supported by the followers of ALI. Thus Uthman became the first of the Caliphs to die at the hands of Muslims.

**Wahabi / Wahhabi**    Followers of the movement founded by Muhammad ibn 'Abd al-Wahhab (1703–87) in Arabia. Muhammad al-Wahhab was inspired by the puritanical teachings of Ibn TAYMIYYA and launched a campaign to restore Islam to a form that was stripped of all accretions arising from culture, tradition or mysticism. He opposed the traditional beliefs in saint-veneration, reliance upon intercessionary prayers, the visiting of tombs and the elevation of Muhammad to semi-divine status. He advocated a return to the basics of SHARI'A but supported the right of individual Muslim scholars to go direct to the QUR'AN and HADITH to interpret and understand the Revelation. Consequently he was opposed to the ULAMA who insisted on their sole right to interpret according to FIQH. Muhammad al-Wahhab linked himself with the House of Saud and between them they created the modern state of Saudi Arabia. The term 'Wahabi' is used generically to describe any movement which supports purification of the faith through stripping away cultural accretions including the traditions of Sufism and also believes in the right of independent individual judgment taken direct from the *Qur'an* and the SUNNA of the Prophet. (*See also* AHL AS-SUNNA WA-JAMAAT; DEOBAND; ITJIHAD)

**Wahy**    The state of receptivity or openness in which Muhammad received and communicated the Revelation of the QUR'AN. It is said that there were outer signs such as physical limpness, swooning and ecstasy that accompanied the appearance of a *Qur'anic* utterance. Essentially there are two, sometimes conflicting, views expressed by

Muslims. The first expresses the view that a prophet is merely an ordinary human being who is chosen to hear, understand and communicate. However, many Muslim scholars, including al-GHAZALI, argue that the messengers are special people endowed with a religious sensitivity. They are given special gifts to receive the Revelation and pass it on to others. Those that advance in religion are able to enter into an experience in which they share in the Prophet's understanding of Revelation. (*See also* MUHAMMAD; RASUL; TANZIL)

**Wali** *Lit. a friend of God* (plural *awliya*). Often used to describe those who are believed to have come close to Allah through their constant remembrance and piety. Although the thousands of SUFIS who have lived such lives are often called saints in translation, the term *awliya* is an accurate description of their relationship to Allah in Muslim terms. A *wali* is believed to possess BARAKA or the ability to bless and intervene on the behalf of the petitioner to Allah. Therefore it is believed that places where he lived or died are still inhabited by his spirit and may be used as retreats to develop ones' own closeness to the Divine. His successors are also believed to contain his spiritual power and this has given rise to the SILSILAH that maintains a Sufi order or TARIQA. (*See also* MAZAR)

**Wali, al-** One of the ninety-nine names of Allah that describes His closeness to human beings in that He walks alongside them and will give protection and shelter. (*See also* WALI)

**Waliallah, Shah** (1703–62) A NAQSHBANDI SUFI mystic and scholar who lived in Delhi. A prolific writer and theologian who attempted to reconcile the differences between the esoteric and the exoteric traditions of Islam by reconciling the SHARI'A (law) to the TARIQA (Sufi orders). This was especially important in the Indian subcontinent where any form of mysticism was likely to become influenced by Hindu practices and ideas. Shah Waliallah reformed the Naqshbandi *tariqa* and virtually all subcontinental Muslim strands can demonstrate their lineage back to the influence of the SHAIKH and his sons. The school of DEOBAND arose from the influence of his successors.

**Wasila** A vast liturgical literature of prayers of mediation. In traditional MOSQUES the prayer-call will be followed with a prayer of mediation addressed to Muhammad. *Wasila* describes the honourable position of a man of influence who has proximity to a monarch. He may be called upon for assistance because of his special access to the ruler. It is believed that prayers that bless Muhammad can be used as access to Allah. (*See also* SHAFA'A)

**Watan** *Lit. fatherland*. The term used to describe one's country in Arab nationalism. The appeal of national patriotism exists in some tension with the Islamic ideal of UMMA (community) united through the Revelation and the leadership of Muhammad. Various Muslim revivalists such as Maulana MAWDUDI and Hasan AL-BANNA have argued that loyalty to the nation runs the risk of supplanting Allah's sovereignty unless the state is an Islamic one.

**Wataniyah / Wataniyyah** Patriotism. (*See also* WATAN)

**Wazifa** A term used by followers of a SUFI order to describe the daily office that is given to them by the SHAIKH at the time of initiation. (*See also* BAI'A; DHIKR; MURID; TARIQA)

**Wird** *See* HIZB.

**Wudu / Wuzu** The ritual ablution that is performed before SALAH. The hands, forearms and legs below the knee are washed, whilst the face, mouth and nose are rinsed. This ritual cleansing may take place at home but every MOSQUE traditionally contains running water so that *wudu* may be performed before prayer. If water is not available sand or clean earth may be used as a lesser substitute. (*See also* NIYYAH)

**Wujud** Allah as pure Being rather than a Being, or as the All of All. This is an important concept for Muslim mystics (SUFIS) as human beings also share in being. The spirit is argued to be a part of God's Being and therefore union is possible. *Wujud* is also used to describe the state of oneness attained by a Sufi in the ecstasy of losing all external consciousness. Ibn ARABI declared the doctrine of Unity (*Wahdat al-*

*Wujud*) which stated that all things pre-exist as ideas in the knowledge of God, whence they emanate and eventually return. This statement gave credence to the Sufi quest. (*See also* TARIQA)

**Yahya ben Zakariya** The Muslim name for John the Baptist, believed to be the prophet of God who preceded Jesus. (*See also* ISA; RASUL)

**Yaquta baida** *Lit. white chrysolite.* A description of the Light or innermost reality that Allah creates from Himself at the beginning of creation; often known as the Light of Muhammad. (*See also* HAQQ; NUR; NUR AL-MUHAMMADI)

**Yathrib** *See* AL-MADINAH.

**Yawm ad-din** The Day of Judgment when all human beings will be called before the Throne of Allah for final recompense. There will be a physical resurrection of the dead. It is generally believed that the People of the Book (Jews, Christians and Muslims) will be judged as communities behind their respective prophets. However, after the final balancing of the books, all human souls will eventually find their way to Paradise through God's overriding infinite mercy and compassion. The Judgment will be based on records kept by various angels who have accompanied each human being throughout their lives and on into the grave where it is believed that the balancing of the final judgment continues. Muslims in the grave receive the fruits of ongoing good actions that they performed in their lifetimes such as introducing someone to Islam or building a well where all can benefit. The Day of Judgment is described in the QUR'AN as a violent and terrifying event out of which God finally appears surrounded by angels. (*See also* SHAFA'A)

**Zabur**   The Arabic name for the Book of Psalms that is one of the four revealed scriptures given by Allah to a chosen messenger. It was revealed to the Prophet DAWUD. (*See also* INJIL; QUR'AN; TAWRAH)

**Zaid, ibn Ali**   A grandson of HUSAIN who is claimed to be the fifth IMAM of the SHI'A community by a breakaway movement who became known as the Zaidis. They rebelled against the UMAYYAD and ABBASID dynasties and founded their own dynasty on the Caspian Sea in 864. Another Zaidi state was founded in the Yemen in 893 and lasted until 1963. Zaidi Shi'a Muslims can still be found in the Yemen. (*See also* ISHMAELI)

**Zakah / Zakat**   The third of the five pillars of Islam is the annual payment of welfare obligatory for all Muslims. In the QUR'AN, the obligation to give charity is often linked with prayer as the dual priorities of submission to God. *Zakah* ensures that Islam remains a communal religion with an emphasis on social responsibility and economic justice. The proportion of income that should go to *Zakah* has ranged from culture to culture and so have the collection mechanisms. Very often it is collected in the MOSQUES whose committees ensure that the money goes to worthy Muslim causes. The general rule for the proportion of wealth given in *Zakah* is that it should be one-fortieth of one's extra income over and above that required to maintain a reasonable standard of living. (*See also* HAJJ; RAMADAN; SADAQAH, SALAH; SHAHADAH)

**Zakat ul-Fitr**    The customary almsgiving observed at the end of the month of fasting or RAMADAN. (*See also* ZAKAH)

**Zalama**    To sin in the sense of self-wrongdoing. Muhammad often began his prayers 'I have wronged myself.' It is typical of Muslim private devotion to ask for forgiveness of such sins which are usually associated with hubris or pride. (*See also* DU'A)

**Zamzam**    The name of the spring which miraculously appeared to save HAJAR and ISHMAEL as an answer to Hajar's prayers for God's assistance. The discovery of the spring allowed MAKKAH to develop as a stopping-off point for merchant caravans. The well was supposed to have been filled in by invaders as a punishment for idol worship in the city but was rediscovered by a devout monotheist who was an ancestor of Muhammad. The spring is believed to be the well adjacent to the *Ka'aba* and is bathed in by the pilgrims who attend the HAJJ.

**Zawiya / Zawiyah**    *Lit. a corner.* It can be used to describe a small MOSQUE, a tomb of a holy man, a cell used by a SUFI for retreat or small Sufi community sharing the same spiritual discipline. It is most commonly used in North Africa to describe a centre of a Sufi order. (*See also* DARGAH; KHANQAH; TARIQA)

**Zikhr**    *See* DHIKR.

**Zimmi**    *See* DHIMMI.

**Ziyarat**    A religious event in which a tomb of a deceased holy man, SUFI or IMAM is visited, usually in order to petition the Divine through the saint's ability to intervene. The petitions are typically pragmatic such as helping in a family problem, or curing sickness or infertility. (*See also* DARGAH; MAZAR)

**Zuhr (Salat ul-Zuhr)**    The second of the five obligatory daily prayers; it can be performed from soon after midday until afternoon. (*See also* ASR; FAJR; ISHA; MAGHRIB; SALAH)